ALL
JEWISH
COOKBOOK

ALL JEWISH COOKBOOK

TEXT WRITTEN BY
JACK A. GHENE

PHOTOGRAPHER:
BART DAVITO

HOME ECONOMIST:
VIVIENNE SPINOZA

 CHARTWELL BOOKS INC.

Published by Chartwell Books Inc.
A Division of Book Sales Inc.
110 Enterprise Avenue
Secaucus, New Jersey 07094

This edition
Published by Chartwell Books Inc.
A Division of Book Sales Inc.
110 Enterprise Avenue
Secaucus, New Jersey 07094

First published 1979
by Paul Hamlyn Pty Limited
176 South Creek Road, Dee Why West, NSW, Australia 2099
© Copyright Paul Hamlyn Pty Limited 1979
Produced in Australia by the Publisher
Typeset in Australia by Terrey Hills Typesetters
Printed by Toppan Printing Co. (Singapore) (Pte) Limited
38 Lui Fang Road, Jurong, Singapore 22.

ISBN: 0-89009-221-4

PREFACE

WHEN one refers to cuisine or cookery one usually means foods that have a national flavor or concept. Hence, French, Italian, Russian, Spanish or Indian cookery reflects the foods and methods of preparation indigenous to a particular country.

What happens when you come to Jewish cookery? It is both interesting and unusual. For almost two thousand years the Jews were without a homeland. Their nomadic wanderings since the Diaspora, dispersed them in many and varied countries. They settled in European countries, in the near East, in the Far East, in Africa and in most countries throughout the world.

The Jews took with them, wherever they went, a set of Biblical instructions regarding diet, the laws of Kashruth. These laws regarding food remain to this day. These instructions and prohibitions influenced what foods Jews were permitted to eat and how they prepared them. Despite the privations the Jews suffered, the physical difficulties they endured and the prejudices they met, they managed to sustain themselves with the foods that were available.

The Old Testament set forth specific instructions regarding dietary patterns for Jews to follow. Orthodox Jews today still adhere to these laws. Many modern Jews are unaware that these laws are part of the Bible and can be found in Leviticus, in Exodus and in Deuteronomy. Adherence to these laws is a personal preference. Today much has changed in the area of food hygiene, and many Jews believe strict adherence to the dietary laws is no longer necessary.

Jewish history is celebrated by holidays and festivals, some of which are religious but most are based on history and tradition. Special foods are served at these times, and religious observances are combined with enjoyment of food. The pre-Sabbath meal is one of the best examples of this: challah, gefilte fish and chicken soup are served and then the event is blessed with wine. The prohibition against cooking on the Sabbath produced a one-dish meal called 'cholent' that is still a favorite with Orthodox Jews.

A variety of other holidays and festivals signal the preparation and serving of special traditional dishes. Such holidays include Rosh Hashana, Sukkoth, Simchas Torah, Chanukah, Chamishasah Bishvat, Shabuoth, Passover and Purim. Each of these occasions are celebrated with specially prepared dishes. For instance, during Passover the Jews celebrate their escape from Egypt when they were forced to bake bread by the heat of the sun. This was unleavened bread and hence matzo is eaten to celebrate Passover. Passover commemorates the deliverence of the Hebrews from Egyptian bondage and is a festival of freedom. The occasion is celebrated with a seder and a service that is combined with the drinking of wine and the partaking of specially prepared foods to remind the Jews of this historic event.

Other holidays and festivals have preferred foods for these special occasions. For instance, Sukkoth features stuffed cabbage; Shabuoth features dairy foods like blintzes and cheese cake; Purim highlights Hamantaschen filled with poppy seeds or prune preserves; Chanukah is celebrated with potato pancakes (latkes).

In a book on Jewish cookery it is helpful to know the original dietary guidelines. The laws of Kashruth specify what foods are kosher and can be eaten, the methods of slaughter, and how to keep a kosher kitchen. The Orthodox Jews are forbidden to mix meat and dairy foods. They are instructed to keep two sets of dishes, one for meat products, the other for dairy products. Pork or pork products, fish that do not have scales, all shellfish and certain types of fowl are prohibited.

Animals and birds must be slaughtered in accordance with the laws. A man specially trained in the methods of slaughter, a shochet, is in charge of this procedure. He uses a special knife, a chaluf, to cut the jugular vein, thus inflicting the minimum of pain on the animal or bird. This method also produces the maximum draining of blood. After slaughter, according to kosher laws, the meat must be koshered before cooking. This is done by soaking and salting the meat to remove any remaining blood.

CONTENTS

INTRODUCTION

MY mother considered herself a good cook. Like so many Jewish mothers, what she lacked in imagination she made up for in quantity. She had learned well from her mother, but neither of them gave much heed to measures or written recipes. 'Watch what I'm doing and you will remember.' So, my mother's and grandmother's meals were limited in variety and shortchanged in inventiveness. I decided there must be more to Jewish cooking than gedempte fleish and overcooked chicken. I believed that carrots and stringbeans and peas could have individual tastes, and I was determined to find out what these tastes were.

This book is the result of that quest and my attempt to bring Jewish cooking into the realm of creative, imaginative dining. And I came to the conclusion that even with Jewish cooking, heartburn does not have to be an aftermath of luncheon or dinner.

From the very outset I realized that one of the major facets of meal planning—and this applies to the cuisines of every people and culture—was the ability to combine a variety of foods. A meal must be planned so that its elements complement each other and make the whole meal enjoyable. Today we know a great deal about nutrition, and we are also diet-conscious, so a meal should not stuff you like the proverbial goose before it goes to slaughter.

Meals should include a variety of foods that are soothing to the palate and nutritionally balanced. But today's dining demands more than this. We have become color-conscious and any meal set before us which is off-white or drab grey, or is covered by a monotone gravy or sauce, leaves us wondering . . . and fearful. To bring Jewish cooking into our present-day milieu I have tried to strike a careful balance between nutrition, color and creativity. And I hope I have accomplished this objective successfully.

Now, you may wonder what makes any book on Jewish cooking Jewish. It's a good question. One of the great experiences that man enjoys is travel, particularly travel abroad. The opportunities to eat different foods and to enjoy different cuisines, accompanied by different national customs, are richly rewarding. Jewish cooking spans a variety of different cultures and nationalities. The Jews have wandered from country to country since the Diaspora, and wherever they settled they adopted some of the foods of that region. As a result, the Jews from eastern Europe developed a series of dishes based on what was eaten in that area. The Jews in southern Europe did the same. Jews who migrated to western Europe, northern Europe, Africa, South America did likewize. As a result, Jewish cooking includes many different ethnic dishes.

My primary desire has been to produce a group of menus which include both traditional and modern Jewish dishes, which are nutritionally balanced, visually interesting and heartburn-free. I have judiciously tried to tread a middle course between kosher cooking and non-kosher cooking, and I have excluded pork, pork products and shellfish from these recipes. I have also avoided menus in which meat products and dairy products are combined. Margarine has been used instead of butter in meat menus. Orthodox Jews may wish to substitute kosher margarine and gelatin. Thus this recipe book will be just as useful to Orthodox Jews as non-Orthodox Jews.

I have presented Jewish cooking in a special menu format in order to make meal-planning easier. By presenting a complete menu rather than individual dishes I hope to make it easier for you to buy, prepare and serve a meal.

The key to a successful meal, whether it is luncheon or dinner, is good menu planning. First read the recipes, then list the necessary ingredients on your shopping list and purchase foods before you start cooking. By planning total meals I have tried to make your task easier.

I hope you enjoy it.

Jack A. Ghene

WINES
TO ENHANCE
DINING PLEASURE

Wine that maketh glad the heart of man.
Psalms, 104:15

WINE enhances food as charm enriches personality. For centuries history has recorded the pleasures that wine adds to the enjoyment of food. Chefs and cooks continue to sing the praises of wines used in cooking. In many situations it makes the difference between good cooking and great cooking.

Right now, however, we are interested in discussing wine as a part of dining enjoyment. For those who follow orthodox Judaism the only wine that may be drunk or used in cooking is kosher wine. This limits the spectrum of what is available. Nevertheless, there are a variety of wines to choose from. These include concord, sweet, medium dry, dry, extra heavy Malaga, sauterne, burgundy and rosé. There are also fruit wines, which are actually dessert wines: blackberry, cherry, elderberry and loganberry. And finally, the sparkling wines: champagne, pink champagne, sparkling burgundy and sparkling concord.

For those who enjoy Jewish cooking but are not limited by the dietary laws of Kashruth, the choice of wines is enormous. Wines can be divided into three main groups: table wines, fortified wines and sparkling wines. Table wines can be red, white or pink and run the gamut from sweet to dry. Most of them are dry, which means they are not sweet. Their alcoholic content is about 13 percent. Fortified wines usually have had a small amount of brandy added so they retain a small amount of natural grape sugar. These are generally called dessert wines and include port and sherry. Their alcoholic content is about 20 percent. Sparkling wines are bubbly or effervescent. Champagne and sparkling burgundy fall into this category.

Chablis and White Burgundy
Color and flavor: Pale yellow, dry; Chablis is flinty.
When to serve: With fish; through a meal.
Temperature: Cold.

Champagne
Color and flavor: Pale to amber, dry, slightly sweet or sweet.
When to serve: With fish; through a meal.
Temperature: Dry: chilled or iced; Sweet: thoroughly iced.

Chianti (red) and Chianti Bianco (white)
Color and flavor: Usually ruby, light and somewhat similar to claret. White, known as Chianti Bianco.
When to serve: Same as claret. White Chianti often served with fish or through a meal.
Temperature: Red: at room temperature; White: slightly chilled.

Claret (Red Bordeaux)
Color and flavor: Usually ruby, light and fine bouquet.
When to serve: With roast (red meats), with chicken, with cold meats or salad; through a meal.
Temperature: At room temperature.

Graves (white) (White Bordeaux)
Color and flavor: Pale yellow or pale golden.
When to serve: With fish; through a meal.
Temperature: Cold.

Liqueurs and Brandy
Color and flavor: Color varies with the type; brandy, amber. Rich, sweet and syrupy.
When to serve: After dessert with coffee.
Temperature: At room temperature.

Madeira
Color and flavor: Amber to reddish brown. slightly sweet or sweet.
When to serve: Dry: with clear soups; Sweet: with desserts.
Temperature: At room temperature.

Muscatel, Marsala and Malaga
Color and flavor: Mostly amber. Sweet, varying in degrees of sweetness.
When to serve: With dessert.
Temperature: At room temperature.

Port
Ruby to tawny. Sweet, full flavored and rather heavy.
When to serve: After dessert.
Temperature: At room temperature.

Red Burgundy
Color and flavor: Dark red, full-bodied, rich bouquet.
When to serve: With roast.
Temperature: At room temperature.

Rhine, Moselle and Alsace
Color and flavor: Usually pale golden or pale yellow. Dry or slightly sweet.
When to serve: With fish or light meats; through a meal.
Temperature: Slightly chilled.

Sauternes and Barsac (White Bordeaux)
Color and flavor: Pale to golden. Slightly sweet or sweet.
When to serve: With dessert or fruit.
Temperature: Medium-sweet: cold; Sweet: very cold.

Sherry
Color and flavor: Amber to delicate brown. Dry, or sweet, nutty, aromatic.
When to serve: Dry: as an appetizer; with clear soups; Sweet: with dessert.
Temperature: Dry: slightly chilled; Sweet: at room temperature.

Vermouth
Color and flavor: French: pale yellow, dry aromatic. Italian: amber, bitter-sweet, aromatic.
When to serve: As an appetizer and in cocktails.
Temperature: Cold.

TRADITIONAL
& HOLIDAY
DISHES

*A man hath no better thing under
the sun, than to eat, and drink,
and to be merry.*

Ecclesiastes, 8:15

THE Jewish calendar is peppered with religious and traditional
festivals, celebrated with a multitude of exciting and different
foods. One of the special events comes fifty-two times a year. It is
the Sabbath. Although religious in nature, it highlights the occasion
of giving thanks for the day of rest, when toil, care, grief and sorrow
are forbidden. The Friday evening, Erev Shabbat, which ushers in
this holy day is the occasion of a festive meal shared by the entire
family. It features: the lighting of candles, prayers, and a feast with
challah, gefilte fish, chicken soup, compote, cake and tea.

There are a host of other holidays, each with special foods to
crown their glory. The New Year, Rosh Hashana, features soup,
brisket, tzimmes, honey cake, vegetables and a beverage, tea or
coffee. The Day of Atonement, Yom Kippur, has a special break-
the-fast menu. It is a light meal that includes eggs, cheeses and cold
fish.

Another series of festivals includes the Feast of Tabernacles,
Sukkoth. It celebrates the harvest gathering and thanks are given for
bountiful crops. Foods served include stuffed breast of veal, soup,
sweet potatoes, cake and beverages.

Chanukah commemorates the rededication of the Temple and
the victory of the Maccabees over the Syrians. The occasion is called
The Festival of Lights. It's a great holiday for children who receive
gifts and enjoy eating potato latkes (pancakes). Some of the foods
that get special attention are stuffed cabbage, roast capon with
stuffing, vegetables and pastry, among a variety of other foods.

13

Chamishasah Bishvat is a traditional holiday that stresses the desire to return to Palestine. It is a tree-planting holiday. The menu features date-nut bread sandwiches, cakes, cookies and nuts.

Purim, the Feast of Lots, is a holiday when gifts are exchanged with relatives and friends. It is a happy occasion and the main food eaten is Hamantaschen, a three-cornered cake filled with poppy seed or prune preserves.

Pesach or Passover is both a feast of freedom and a spring farm festival. It is a reminder of the deliverence of the Jews from bondage in Egypt. A seder, a special kind of meal, is eaten during the reading and chanting of the Haggadah that ushers in this occasion. The privations that the Jews suffered in Egypt are recalled in the eating of matzo (unleavened bread) and a variety of special foods which are not eaten at any other time of the year.

Cholent

¼ cup chicken fat
½ lb dried lima beans
1½ lb stewing or soup meat
1 onion, finely cut
2 tablespoons flour
1 teaspoon salt
freshly ground pepper
⅛ cup ground ginger
small piece of bay leaf
3 lb potatoes, thickly sliced
paprika
1½ cups water

1 Grease the bottom of a pot (preferably an iron one) with some chicken fat.
2 Wash beans in boiling water and add to the pot.
3 Add meat.
4 Mix onion thoroughly with flour, seasonings and bay leaf.
5 Place a layer of potatoes on meat.
6 Sprinkle with some of the flour mixture and repeat with a layer of potatoes and a sprinkling of the flour mixture until both are used.
7 Add remaining chicken fat and a little paprika
8 Add 1½ cups of water, pouring it carefully down the side of the pot.
9 Bring to the boil on top of the stove.
10 Cover tightly and place in a pre-heated oven at 400°F for ½ hour.
11 Turn heat down low and keep pot tightly covered.
12 Keep on low heat overnight or all day, until ready to serve.

Kreplach

1 cup flour
2 eggs, beaten

Filling
1 lb ground cooked meat
1 egg
1 onion, finely cut (optional)
seasonings

1 Sift flour, make a mound, scoop out a hole and drop in beaten eggs.
2 Fold eggs into flour until dough is easy to handle. Work until smooth.
3 Roll out to ¼ inch thickness. Cut into 2½ inch squares.
4 Mix filling ingredients together.
5 Fill squares with prepared meat filling. Seal edges.
6 Drop squares into boiling salted water and cook for about 20 minutes.
7 Drain and serve in soup.

Gefilte Fish

Serves 6

1 lb onions
3-4 lb freshwater fish fillets
½ teaspoon pepper
1 tablespoon salt
1 tablespoon matzo meal
½ cup water
3 eggs, well beaten

Stock
1 bay leaf
dash allspice
2 onions, chopped
2 stalks celery, chopped

1 Chop onions finely and place into a wooden bowl.
2 Chop the fish finely (for the best results use two varieties of freshwater fish, such as whitefish and yellow pike).
3 Add pepper, salt and matzo meal.
4 Mix thoroughly, adding water and eggs a little at a time. (Do not allow the mixture to become too soft to handle.)
5 Make mixture into patties, and drop into a large pot of boiling water (2 quarts or more), to which the stock ingredients have been added.
6 Boil for ½ hour over a high heat, taking care not to let it burn. Reduce heat to low and boil for 1 hour longer.
7 Drain fish patties. Cool and serve with crisp parsley and horseradish.

Carrot Tzimmes with Knoedel

2 lb stew beef
1 quart water
4 carrots, scraped and grated
2 sweet potatoes, sliced
2 potatoes, sliced
2 tablespoons sugar

Knoedel
2 eggs, well beaten
1 teaspoon sugar
salt and pepper
$\frac{1}{2}$ cup shortening
$\frac{1}{4}$ cup warm water
$\frac{3}{4}$ cup matzo meal

1 Cook meat in 1 quart of water for 1 hour.
2 Add carrots, potatoes and sugar and cook until tender.
3 Combine knoedel ingredients.
4 Chill in refrigerator for 10 minutes.
5 Add to meat and vegetables in the pot.
6 Cook until light and tender.

Sunday Pudding

1 egg
$\frac{3}{4}$ cup sugar
3 tablespoons flour
$1\frac{1}{4}$ teaspoons baking powder
$\frac{1}{8}$ teaspoon salt
$\frac{1}{2}$ cup chopped nuts
$\frac{1}{2}$ cup chopped apples
1 teaspoon vanilla

1 Beat egg well.
2 Add sugar and beat until light and creamy.
3 Sift flour, baking powder and salt and add to egg mixture.
4 Fold in nuts, apples and vanilla and blend thoroughly.
5 Pour into a greased 9 inch pan.
6 Bake at 325°F for about 30 minutes.
7 Serve with ice cream or whipped cream.

Tzimmes

Serves 8

2 lb sweet potatoes or yams
2 medium carrots, parboiled
1 lb prunes, washed
$2\frac{1}{2}$ cups pineapple pieces
1 teaspoon salt
brown sugar to taste
pineapple juice from can

1 Peel sweet potatoes or yams; cut into $1\frac{1}{2}$ inch slices.
2 Cut carrots into 1 inch pieces.
3 Arrange sweet potatoes, carrots, prunes and pineapple in an oblong pan.
4 Sprinkle with salt and sugar and pour over pineapple juice.
5 Bake in a pre-heated oven at 400°F and baste from time to time with pineapple juice.
6 When potatoes and carrots are soft and brown, remove from oven.

Soup Nuts
(Mandlen)

Serves 4

3 eggs
2 cups flour
$\frac{1}{2}$ teaspoon salt
2 tablespoons oil

1 Mix eggs, flour and salt.
2 Put on a floured board.
3 Roll out into a rope shape about 1 inch thick (in the palms of your hands).
4 Cut with knife dipped in flour into $\frac{1}{2}$ inch pieces.
5 Oil baking dish slightly and put cut pieces into baking dish.
6 Bake in a pre-heated oven at 375°F for about 10 minutes or until brown.
7 Shake baking pan in order to brown soup nuts evenly.
8 Use soup nuts as garnish for chicken soup.

Stewed Dried Fruit (see page 63)

Egg Pilau

Serves 8

2 cups rice
salt
4 cups chicken soup
6 eggs
½ cup chicken fat
pepper and paprika to taste

1 Cook rice with salt in chicken soup, keeping the pot tightly covered.
2 The rice will absorb all the soup and should be soft in 20 minutes.
3 Beat the eggs very lightly, add the fat and stir mixture gradually into the rice.
4 Remove from the heat immediately. (The heat of the rice will cook the eggs and melt the fat without returning the pot to the stove.)
5 Season to taste with pepper and paprika.
6 Divide into 8 portions and serve at once with poultry.

Bread Dumplings

1 loaf stale bread
1 medium onion, finely cut
3 tablespoons shortening
2 eggs, lightly beaten
1 tablespoon chopped parsley
¼ teaspoon nutmeg or ginger
½ teaspoon salt
⅛ teaspoon freshly ground pepper

1 Break bread into pieces and soak in water.
2 Squeeze water from bread so that it is not too wet.
3 Brown onion in shortening until golden brown.
4 Stir in the soaked bread until shortening has been absorbed.
5 Put into a bowl and cool.
6 Add eggs, parsley, nutmeg or ginger, salt and pepper.

Sweet and Sour Tongue (see page 59)

7 Shape into balls with lightly floured hands to ease rolling; handle as little as possible.
8 Place on a platter and refrigerate for a few hours, or overnight.
9 When ready to serve, boil salted water in a large pot.
10 Put dumplings in boiling water and continue to boil until they rise to the top.
11 Remove dumplings, one by one, using a slotted spoon.
12 Place on a platter and serve with meat, such as sweet and sour tongue.

Potato Kugel

2 tablespoons chicken fat
1 onion, chopped
6 potatoes, grated
½ cup flour
½ teaspoon salt
2 eggs

1 Heat fat and brown onion.
2 Combine rest of ingredients, then add cooked onion.
3 Put into a greased pan.
4 Bake for 1 hour at 350°F.
5 Cut into portions and serve.

Cheese Latkes

1 lb cottage cheese
3 eggs
2 tablespoons flour
1 teaspoon sugar
salt and pepper to taste
sour cream for serving

1 Push cheese through a sieve.
2 Mix all ingredients together except sour cream.
3 Drop tablespoons of the batter into a hot, buttered griddle.
4 Fry until latkes are brown on one side, then turn and brown on the other side.
5 Serve with a side dish of sour cream.

BREADS

Challah

Yield 1 loaf

1 cake (1 oz) compressed yeast
¼ cup warm water
5 cups flour
1 teaspoon salt
1 teaspoon sugar
1 tablespoon oil
1 egg
warm water
1 egg, lightly beaten

1 Dissolve yeast in warm water.
2 Combine flour, salt, sugar and oil.
3 Add yeast mixture.
4 Beat egg and add. Add enough warm water to knead smooth.
5 Cover dough and let it rise until it bubbles.
6 Knead again and allow to rise.
7 Roll out into 3 strips and braid.
8 Place in a pan and let mixture rise.
9 Brush with beaten egg yolk before putting in the oven.
10 Bake at 350°F for 1 hour or until golden brown.

Challah

Yield 4 loaves

2 packets dry granular yeast
2½ cups warm water
6 tablespoons sugar
2 teaspoons salt
⅓ cup salad oil
4 eggs
8⅔ cups all-purpose flour
1 egg yolk
1 teaspoon cold water
4 teaspoons poppy seeds

1 Dissolve yeast in warm water in a large bowl.
2 Add sugar, salt, salad oil, eggs and 6 cups flour.
3 Beat thoroughly with a wooden spoon.
4 Gradually add more flour until dough is too stiff to beat with a spoon.
5 Place remaining flour on a pastry board, turn the dough out on top of it and knead until the dough is smooth and all the flour is absorbed.
6 If the dough is still quite sticky, you may add more flour to get the right consistency.
7 Place dough in a large covered bowl and let it rise in a warm place (85°)F for 1½ hours or until it triples in size.
8 Punch dough down and divide into 12 portions.
9 Shape each portion into a rope about 1 inch in diameter.
10 Braid 3 ropes together on a floured board.
11 Repeat with remaining ropes, to make 4 loaves.
12 Place each braid in a well-greased 4½ inch x 8½ inch loaf pan and place in a warm place to rise for ¾ hour or until it almost triples in size.
13 Brush loaf tops with egg yolk mixed with cold water and sprinkle with poppy seeds.
14 Pre-heat oven to 375°F and bake for 25-30 minutes or until bread is golden brown.

Teiglach

2 lb honey
1 cup sugar
4 cups flour
4 eggs
2 teaspoons baking powder
1 teaspoon vinegar
freshly ground salt
1 tablespoon water
½ teaspoon ground ginger
½ cup chopped walnuts
1 cup water

1 Combine honey and sugar and cook over a low heat until mixture boils.
2 Mix flour, eggs, baking powder, vinegar and salt. Add water.
3 Roll out to a soft dough.
4 Roll dough into small pieces about the size of marbles.
5 Drop into honey mixture.
6 Add ginger and cook for ½ hour.
7 Add walnuts and cook until dough balls turn brown.
8 Add 1 cup water and turn off heat.

Hamantaschen

2¼ cups flour
2 teaspoons baking powder
1 teaspoon salt
¼ cup sugar
¼ cup melted butter
1 egg
¾ cup milk

1 Mix flour, baking powder, salt, sugar, butter, egg and milk.
2 Knead dough well and roll out thinly. Cut into 2 inch rounds.
3 If desired place a spoonful of filling such as prunes and chopped nuts in the center of each round.
4 Draw up 3 sides of each round and pinch together to form a triangle.
5 Place on a buttered cookie sheet.
6 Bake for 45-60 minutes at 375°F.

Hot Breads

1 cake (1 oz) yeast
1 cup lukewarm water
½ cup shortening
½ cup boiling water
2 teaspoons salt
½ cup sugar
½ cup cold water
3 eggs, beaten
8½ cups flour

1 Dissolve yeast in lukewarm water.
2 Put shortening in a mixing bowl and pour boiling water over it.
3 Add salt, sugar, cold water and eggs.
4 Add yeast mixture.
5 Add 3 cups of flour and beat.
6 Add 5½ cups of flour.
7 Place in the refrigerator until required.
8 Roll into desired shapes.
9 Allow dough to rise.
10 Bake in a pre-heated oven at 350°F.

Corn Bread

Yield 6 x 4-inch squares

¾ cup flour, sifted
1½ cups yellow cornmeal
4 teaspoons baking powder
1 teaspoon salt
2 tablespoons sugar (optional)
2 eggs, well beaten
1¼ cups milk
¼ cup shortening, melted

1 Sift flours and mix with other dry ingredients. (Sugar may be omitted, if desired.)
2 Combine eggs and milk and add to flour mixture, stirring until well mixed.
3 Stir in shortening.
4 Turn into a greased shallow pan and bake in a pre-heated oven at 400°F for about 30 minutes.

Thin Corn Bread

Serves 6-8

1 cup water-ground cornmeal
1 cup flour
3 teaspoons baking powder
1 tablespoon sugar
1 teaspoon salt
2 eggs, beaten
1½ cups milk
4 tablespoons melted butter

1 Sift together corn meal, flour, baking powder, sugar and salt.
2 Add eggs to milk.
3 Add flour mixture, and beat with a spoon just enough to mix.
4 Stir in melted butter, and spread mixture into 2 round 9-inch tins, which have been well buttered.
5 Bake in a pre-heated oven at 500°F for about 20-30 minutes, until golden brown.
6 Turn out on hot plates, cut in pie-shaped pieces and serve at once.

Muffins

1¾ cups flour, sifted
¾ teaspoon salt
¼ cup sugar
2 teaspoons baking powder
2 tablespoons melted butter
¾ cup milk
2 eggs, beaten

1 Sift dry ingredients.
2 Combine melted butter with milk and add to beaten eggs.
3 Stir the liquid into the dry ingredients in 15-20 seconds—ignore the lumps.
4 Pour the batter at once into greased muffin tins, filling each cup ⅓ full.
5 Bake for 15-20 minutes in the oven at 425°F.
6 When cooked remove at once from tins.

Bran Muffins

1 cup flour
2 teaspoons baking powder
½ teaspoon salt
1 cup All Bran
½ cup milk
½ cup molasses
1 tablespoon sugar
3 tablespoons melted butter
1 egg, beaten
1 cup seedless raisins, soaked

1 Sift flour, baking powder and salt together.
2 Add remaining ingredients.
3 Mix well and put into greased muffin tins.
4 Bake at 350°F for 25 minutes or until golden brown.

Note: This recipe yields about 12 Bran Muffins.

Refrigerator Rolls

1 cake (1 oz) compressed yeast
½ cup lukewarm water
½ cup shortening
1 cup scalded milk
2 eggs, well beaten
⅓ cup sugar
2 teaspoons salt
1 cup mashed potato
5 cups flour (approx.)
melted butter
1 egg, beaten (optional)

1 Dissolve yeast in lukewarm water.
2 Add shortening to scalded milk and cool.
3 Add yeast mixture and mix thoroughly.
4 Add eggs, sugar, salt and potatoes.
5 Add enough flour to make a stiff dough.
6 Turn out on a lightly floured board and knead well.
7 Place in a large, greased bowl.
8 Brush with melted butter.
9 Cover tightly and place in the refrigerator.
10 About 1 hour before baking, punch down dough.

11 Shape desired number of rolls.
12 Brush with melted butter.
13 Let rolls rise until light.
14 If desired, brush with beaten egg.
15 Bake in a pre-heated oven at 425°F for about 15-20 minutes.

Ginger Orange Muffins

2 cups flour
½ teaspoon salt
4 teaspoons baking powder
4 tablespoons sugar
½ teaspoon ground ginger
1 egg
¾ cup milk
4 tablespoons melted butter
grated rind of 2 oranges
ground ginger (for topping)
granulated sugar (for topping)

1 Sift dry ingredients together. Add egg, milk and melted butter.
2 Add grated orange rind. Retain a small amount and mix this with ginger and granulated sugar for topping. Sprinkle over the top of each muffin before it is baked.
3 Bake in the oven at 400°F for 15-20 minutes.

Biscuits Supreme

2 cups flour, sifted
½ teaspoon salt
4 teaspoons baking powder
½ teaspoon cream of tartar
2 teaspoons sugar
½ cup shortening
⅔ cup milk

1 Sift dry ingredients.
2 Work in softened shortening.
3 Add milk all at once and work in quickly.
4 Roll dough out on a lightly floured board till about ½ inch thick.

5 Cut with a biscuit cutter.
6 Bake on a greased sheet in a pre-heated oven at 425°F for about 15 minutes.

Potato Gem Muffins

1 cake (1 oz) compressed yeast
¼ teaspoon salt
1 teaspoon sugar
1 cup warm water
1 cup mashed potato
2 tablespoons fat
1 egg, beaten
2 – 2½ cups all purpose flour

1 Dissolve yeast cake with salt and sugar in water.
2 Add potatoes, fat, egg and flour. Mix well.
3 Stand aside to allow mixture to rise.
4 Cut down dough and drop spoonfuls of mixture into greased muffin tins.
5 Allow muffins to rise again before placing in oven.
6 Bake in a pre-heated oven at 450°F for 15-20 minutes.

Onion Crackers

3 cups flour
1 teaspoon baking powder
3 large onions, finely diced
3 eggs, well beaten
3 oz oil
1 tablespoon sugar
1½ tablespoons salt

1 Sift flour and baking powder together.
2 Mix all ingredients together, adding enough flour to roll.
3 Knead lightly.
4 Roll dough out thinly.
5 Cut into rounds.
6 Bake in a pre-heated oven at 350°F until browned.

Parkerhouse Rolls

1 cake (1 oz) compressed yeast
4 tablespoons sugar
1 cup lukewarm milk
4 cups flour, sifted
1½ teaspoons salt
4 tablespoons shortening
1 egg, beaten
melted butter

1 Crumble yeast into a mixing bowl and add sugar.
2 Add lukewarm milk.
3 Stir well to mix ingredients thoroughly.
4 Add 2 cups flour and the salt. Mix well.
5 Add melted shortening and beaten egg.
6 Beat the batter thoroughly and gradually add the remainder of the flour.
7 Remove the dough to a floured board and knead for 5-10 minutes until it is smooth and elastic.
8 Cover with a cloth and let the dough rise until it doubles in size.
9 With a small biscuit cutter cut the dough into rounds. Crease the rolls at one side with the blunt side of a knife.
10 Brush with melted butter and fold over. Place rolls apart to prevent them from touching.
11 Allow rolls to rise until double in size.
12 Bake in a pre-heated oven at 400°F for 15-20 minutes.

Date Bread

1 teaspoon baking soda
1½ cups boiling water
1 lb dates, chopped
3 tablespoons butter
2 eggs
1 cup sugar
2 cups flour, sifted

1 Add soda to boiling water. Pour over dates and add butter.
2 When cool, add other ingredients.
3 Pour into a bread tin and bake for about 50 minutes in a moderate oven.

SALAD
DRESSINGS & RELISHES

French Dressing

¼ teaspoon paprika
1 teaspoon dry mustard
½ cup sugar
1½ teaspoons salt
1 can tomato soup
1½ cups salad oil
¾ cup vinegar
2 tablespoons Worcestershire sauce
2 teaspoons onion juice

1 Mix dry ingredients together.
2 Add liquid ingredients.
3 Shake thoroughly and serve.

Russian Dressing

½ cup mayonnaise
¼ cup Indian relish
¼ cup chili sauce
½ teaspoon powdered sugar

1 Mix ingredients together well.
2 Serve cold.

Viennese Dressing

3 hard-cooked eggs
¾ cup thin sour cream
½ cup tarragon vinegar

1 tablespoon sugar
1 teaspoon salt
1 teaspoon prepared mustard

1 Press egg yolks through a coarse strainer. Finely chop egg whites and set aside.
2 Mix egg yolks and other ingredients and blend well. (The mixture should be almost as thin as coffee cream.)
3 Pour dressing over salad greens in a bowl. Garnish with finely chopped egg whites.

Herb Dressing

French Dressing
1 tablespoon finely chopped fresh mint
1 tablespoon finely chopped fresh tarragon
1 tablespoon finely chopped fresh parsley
1 tablespoon finely chopped chives

1 Combine herbs with French Dressing.
2 Chill and serve.

Thousand Island Dressing

3 hard-cooked eggs
1 medium onion
1 medium green pepper
3 canned pimientos
1 cup mayonnaise
½ cup catsup
salt to taste

1 Put eggs, onion, green pepper and pimientos through a food chopper or processor.
2 Add mayonnaise and catsup.
3 Serve dressing with lettuce.

Cole Slaw Dressing

1 teaspoon salt
¼ teaspoon paprika
⅛ teaspoon white pepper
½ cup vinegar
½ cup sweetened condensed milk

1 Blend spices in vinegar.
2 Slowly add vinegar to condensed milk and stir until thoroughly blended.
3 Serve dressing with about 3 cups of finely shredded or chopped new white cabbage. (Cabbage should be soaked in ice-cold water for 1 hour, drained and dried before dressing is added.)

Cole Slaw Boiled Dressing

2 eggs, lightly beaten
½ cup vinegar
3 tablespoons olive oil
salt and pepper
½ cup sugar
1 teaspoon dry mustard

1 Mix all ingredients together in a saucepan.
2 Put on the stove to cook, stirring constantly.
3 Remove from heat and mix dressing with shredded cabbage.
4 Allow salad to stand for a couple of hours before serving.

Celery Seed Dressing

1 tablespoon sugar
1 teaspoon dry mustard

1 teaspoon salt
1 onion, grated
1 cup oil
½ cup vinegar
¼ cup celery seed

1 Mix all ingredients together except vinegar and celery seed. Beat thoroughly.
2 Slowly add vinegar.
3 Add celery seed.
Note: Celery Seed Dressing is excellent with any fruit salad.

Sour Cream Dressing

1 cup sour cream
½ cup mayonnaise
1 teaspoon lemon juice
¼ teaspoon dry mustard
1 tablespoon horseradish
dash cayenne pepper
salt
dash paprika
2 teaspoons chopped chives
1 teaspoon onion juice

1 Blend ingredients together thoroughly.
2 Chill dressing and serve very cold.

Roquefort Dressing

½ cup salad oil
2 tablespoons wine vinegar
2 tablespoons lemon juice
½ teaspoon salt
½ teaspoon celery seed
⅛ teaspoon pepper
½ teaspoon sugar
½ teaspoon paprika
⅓ cup Roquefort cheese, crumbled

1 Combine all ingredients in a jar with a tight lid and shake well.
2 Refrigerate.
3 Shake again before serving.

Roquefort Cheese Dressing

2 tablespoons mayonnaise
3 tablespoons Roquefort cheese, crumbled
French Dressing
½ teaspoon Worcestershire sauce

1 Mix mayonnaise and cheese together.
2 Mix in French Dressing very slowly;
   then add Worcestershire sauce.

Watercress Dressing

1½ teaspoons dry mustard
1 teaspoon paprika
1½ teaspoons sugar
1½ teaspoons salt
¼ teaspoon pepper
⅓ cup vinegar
1 cup olive oil
1 clove garlic, crushed
dash Worcestershire sauce
1 teaspoon chili sauce
dash Tabasco sauce
5 tablespoons chopped watercress

1 Combine all ingredients except watercress.
2 Mix with an electric beater for about 3
   minutes until well blended and slightly
   thick.
3 Stir in watercress and mix thoroughly.
Note: Watercress Dressing is excellent with
meat or a vegetable or green salad.

Chiffonade Dressing

2 tablespoons finely chopped parsley
2 tablespoons finely chopped red sweet
pepper
1 teaspoon finely chopped shallots or
onion
2 hard-cooked eggs, finely chopped
French Dressing

1 Mix ingredients together.
2 Chill.
3 Shake vigorously before serving.

Horseradish Sauce

2 tablespoons margarine
2 tablespoons flour
1 cup beef stock
2 tablespoons horseradish
chopped parsley
dash dill (optional)

1 Melt margarine.
2 Stir in flour.
3 Add stock and cook until mixture
   thickens.
4 Add horseradish, parsley and dill.
Note: Horseradish Sauce can be served with
boiled or corned beef.

Chantilly Dressing

3 tablespoons confectioners' sugar
fruit juice
1 cup mayonnaise
½ cup sweet or sour cream

1 Blend sugar with a little fruit juice.
2 Add mayonnaise and cream. Blend again.

Fruit Salad Dressing

¼ cup each of orange, lemon and pineapple
   juice
¼ cup water
¼ cup honey
3 eggs, lightly beaten
whipped cream (optional)

1 Heat the fruit juices, water and honey.
2 Add the beaten eggs and cook until mixture has thickened.
3 Whipped cream may be added just before serving.

Fruity Dressing

juice of 1 orange
juice of 1 lemon
1 cup salad oil
1 tablespoon vinegar
⅓ cup sugar
1 teaspoon salt
1 teaspoon paprika
1 teaspoon grated onion
½ teaspoon celery seed

1 Combine all ingredients.
2 Blend thoroughly before serving.

Honey Fruit Dressing

1 cup lemon juice
½ cup honey
½ cup sugar
2 teaspoons dry mustard
2 teaspoons salt
½ tablespoons grated lemon rind
¼ cup orange juice
2 cups salad oil

1 Mix ½ cup lemon juice with all ingredients except salad oil.
2 Add salad oil and stir constantly.
3 Add remaining ½ cup lemon juice and continue stirring for few more seconds.

Raisin Sauce

½ cup seedless raisins
cold water

2 small onions, sliced and sautéed in butter
½ cup catsup
salt and pepper
dash sugar
dash ground ginger
6 gingersnaps
2 tablespoons lemon juice or vinegar
2 cups water
blanched slivered almonds
1 teaspoon cornstarch

1 Soak seedless raisins in cold water and drain.
2 Combine all ingredients except raisins, almonds and cornstarch.
3 Bring to the boil and simmer until mixture thickens.
4 Add blanched slivered almonds and soaked raisins.
5 Cook for 15 minutes longer.
6 If sauce is not thick enough, add 1 teaspoon cornstarch which has been mixed in a little cold water.

Whipped Orange Butter

½ lb margarine
1 cup fine sugar
2 oz orange juice concentrate
1 oz Cointreau or Triple Sec
2 oz light honey
grated rind of 1 orange

1 Mix margarine and sugar at low speed with an electric beater.
2 Add orange juice concentrate, liqueur, honey and orange rind.
3 Increase speed of beater. Mixture will almost double in size.
4 Store at room temperature in a covered dish until required.
5 Butter will keep for 5-6 days.
Note: Recipe makes about 1 pint of Whipped Orange Butter. Delicious on hot breads, corn bread or muffins.

Sweet Mayonnaise

4 egg yolks
2 tablespoons sugar
4 tablespoons vinegar
3 tablespoons water
1 tablespoon flour
1 tablespoon butter
salt to taste
½-1 cup cream, whipped
½ teaspoon dry mustard

1 Beat egg yolks.
2 Add sugar. Add remaining ingredients except cream.
3 Put mixture in a saucepan and cook slowly until it begins to thicken.
4 Cool and add whipped cream.

Note: This is a perfect dressing for chicken salad and fruit salads.

Never Fail Mayonnaise

½ teaspoon dry mustard
½ teaspoon salt
½ teaspoon sugar
dash cayenne pepper
2 egg yolks, lightly beaten
1½ tablespoons cold water
1-1½ cups salad oil
1 tablespoon vinegar

1 Mix dry ingredients together.
2 Add to egg yolks.
3 Add water, then beat in oil drop by drop until liquid is thick.
4 Add vinegar.

Pepper Relish

2 heads cabbage (about 5 lb)
8 carrots
8 green peppers
12 onions
½ cup salt
2½ pints vinegar
6 cups sugar
1 teaspoon celery seed
1 teaspoon mustard seed

1 Grind cabbage, carrots, peppers and onions in a food chopper.
2 Add salt and stand aside for 2 hours.
3 Drain, pressing out as much liquid as possible.
4 Add remaining ingredients, mixing well.
5 Put into jars.

Note: Pepper Relish will keep without sealing.

Baba Marsha's Pickles

4 quarts (16 cups) medium cucumbers
3 cups sugar
2½ cups vinegar
1 teaspoon celery seed
4 small onions, sliced
½ cup prepared mustard
4 teaspoons salt
1 teaspoon turmeric

1 Wash and slice cucumbers and put into 4 quart jars.
2 Mix other ingredients together and bring to the boil.
3 Pour over cucumbers. Can and seal.
4 Allow cucumber pickles to stand for 6 weeks before use.

Garlic Pickles

12 large cucumbers
4½ cups cold water
½ cup salt
3 cups vinegar
1½ cups brown sugar
6 cloves garlic, crushed
12 teaspoons horseradish
6 teaspoons mustard seed
6 small hot peppers

1 Halve the cucumbers and quarter them (so they will fit into pint jars).
2 Soak cucumbers in cold water and salt overnight.
3 Drain.
4 Combine vinegar and brown sugar. Add cucumbers and heat thoroughly, but do not boil.
5 Prepare jars and divide seasoning among them, add scalded cucumbers and seal.

Pressed Cucumber

1 large cucumber
$\frac{1}{3}$ cup vinegar
$\frac{1}{3}$ cup water
$\frac{1}{2}$ teaspoon sugar
dash pepper
$\frac{1}{2}$ teaspoon salt
1 sprig parsley, finely cut

1 Peel cucumber and slice thinly.
2 Spread slices out evenly in a pie plate.
3 Put another empty pie plate on top so that it fits inside the first one, on top of the cucumber.
4 Use both hands and press hard on the top pie plate, so that the cucumber slices are squeezed between the two plates.
5 Press until cucumber becomes watery.
6 Mix remaining ingredients thoroughly.
7 Pour over the pressed cucumber in the pie plate.
8 Transfer to a deep covered dish and refrigerate until required.

Tomato Relish

1 peck (32 cups) ripe tomatoes
2 cups sliced celery
1 quart vinegar
2 lb brown sugar
$\frac{1}{2}$ cup white mustard seed
2 cups chopped onions
4 sweet green peppers
1 cup salt (not iodized)
1 cup prepared horseradish
1 teaspoon black pepper

1 Wash tomatoes.
2 Scald in hot water, slip off skins, remove stem ends and any blemishes.
3 Cut into small pieces, place in colander or cheesecloth bag and drain for several hours or overnight.
4 Mix drained tomatoes with remaining ingredients and place in a sterilized crock.
5 Cover and stand for several days, stirring occasionally.
6 Tomato Relish may be kept indefinitely in a covered crock, or can be stored in sterilized jars.

LUNCHEON
MENUS

*It is the part of a wise man to feed himself with moderate
pleasant food and drink, and to take pleasure with
perfumes, with the beauty of growing plants, dress, music,
sports and theatres, and other places of this kind which
man may use without any hurt to his fellows.*

Spinoza

PHILOSOPHERS, poets, noblemen and plain mortals like you
and me have always enjoyed the experience of dining.

These luncheon menus, like the dinners, are offered as complete
scenarios. You create the characters. You give them value, vitality
and exuberance. The lunch menus differ from the dinners in that
they are lighter. They may also be served as suppers, if you wish.
Jewish meals need not be heavy or gross. These luncheon menus are
not meant to be unalterable. They are presented in a format that
offers you ideas and alternatives. You may make changes and
substitutions, but be careful to maintain a balanced meal.

Jews have travelled widely and have adopted foods and cuisines
from many places. This variety makes eating at the Jewish table an
international event. You can serve French, Italian, Spanish, Russian
and Hungarian dishes with a 'Jewish twist'. And these menus
prove that Jewish foods need never be dull. Our eating habits are
changing and, as a result, we offer you 'and/or' choices in these
luncheon menus. If the occasion calls for it, and you feel so inclined,
gourmandise. Otherwise, take the alternate route. Omit the
additional items. Whatever you do, enjoy what you eat!

LUNCHEON

Menu

No. 1

Serves 6

Clear Broth
and/or
Mushroom-stuffed Tomatoes

Brisket of Beef

Cucumber Salad

Pineapple Relish

Braised Celery with Almonds
and/or
Potato Latkes
(Pancakes)

Jelly Roll

Coffee or Tea

Clear Broth

3 lb shin of beef
3 quarts cold water
$\frac{1}{8}$ teaspoon salt
$\frac{1}{8}$ teaspoon freshly ground pepper

1 Cut beef into pieces. Remove fat.
2 Add water, salt and pepper. Partly cover and bring slowly to boiling point.
3 Simmer gently for 5 hours or until cooked, removing scum as it forms.
4 Keep meat well covered with water.
5 Remove meat, cool, and skim off the fat.
6 Strain the cooking liquid carefully through a fine sieve or cheesecloth.
7 Reheat and serve.

Mushroom-stuffed Tomatoes

6 medium tomatoes
$1\frac{1}{2}$ cups chopped fresh mushrooms
3 tablespoons margarine
$\frac{1}{2}$ cup sour cream substitute
2 egg yolks, beaten
$\frac{1}{4}$ cup fine dry breadcrumbs
1 teaspoon salt
$\frac{1}{8}$ teaspoon pepper
$\frac{1}{8}$ teaspoon thyme
3 tablespoons breadcrumbs (extra)

1 Cut stem end from tomatoes; scoop out pulp.
2 Turn shells upside down to drain.
3 Chop pulp into fine pieces.
4 Set aside 1 cup of pulp.
5 Cook mushrooms in 2 tablespoons margarine until tender.
6 Combine sour cream substitute and egg yolks.
7 Add to mushrooms with tomato pulp; mix well.
8 Stir in the $\frac{1}{4}$ cup breadcrumbs, salt, pepper and thyme.
9 Cook and stir until mixture thickens and boils.
10 Place tomato shells in 10 inch x 6 inch x $1\frac{1}{2}$ inch baking dish.
11 Spoon mushroom mixture into tomatoes.
12 Combine 1 tablespoon melted butter and 3 tablespoons breadcrumbs; sprinkle on top of tomatoes.
13 Bake in a pre-heated oven at 375°F for 25 minutes.
Note: Mushroom-stuffed Tomatoes may be prepared ready for baking and placed in the refrigerator the day before required.

Brisket of Beef

1 packet onion soup mix
1 small bottle ginger ale
1 cup catsup
4-5 lb piece of brisket

1 Combine soup mix, ginger ale and catsup and pour over brisket in a heavy roasting pan.
2 Cover and cook for 2 hours in an oven pre-heated to 375°F. Uncover and cook for 1 hour longer.
3 If gravy dries out, add a small amount of water.
4 Slice across the grain and serve.

Cucumber Salad

2 large cucumbers, peeled and sliced thinly
5 scallions, trimmed and chopped
2 tablespoons vinegar
$\frac{1}{4}$ cup sour cream substitute
salt and black pepper to taste

1 Combine cucumbers and scallions in a mixing bowl.
2 Blend the remaining ingredients.
3 Pour over the vegetables.
4 Toss lightly and chill.

Pineapple Relish

    1 x 1 lb 4 oz can pineapple chunks
    ¼ cup vinegar
    12 whole cloves
    ¼ cup sugar
    coarsely grated rind of 1 lemon
    3 x 3-inch sticks of cinnamon

1 Combine all ingredients.
2 Place in a covered basin or jar and refrigerate for at least seven days.

Braised Cherry with Almonds

    2 tablespoons chopped onion
    2½ cups celery cut diagonally in ½ inch slices
    1 tablespoon margarine
    ¼ can bouillon or consommé
    ⅛ teaspoon salt
    ⅛ teaspoon freshly ground pepper
    ¼ cup chopped roasted unblanched almonds

1 Sauté onion and celery in margarine until lightly browned.
2 Add bouillon or consommé, salt and pepper.
3 Cover and cook until tender and liquid is absorbed.
4 Add chopped almonds and serve.
Note: Braised Celery with Almonds can also be baked in the oven.

Potato Latkes
(Pancakes)

    2 lb new potatoes
    1 medium onion
    2 eggs
    ½ teaspoon baking powder
    1½ teaspoons salt

    dash pepper
    ¼ cup matzo meal
    oil for frying

1 Peel potatoes and onion. Grate or put through a grinder using the fine blade.
2 Mix in eggs, baking powder, salt, pepper and matzo meal.
3 Drop by spoonfuls into hot oil, almost deep enough to cover pancakes.
4 Fry over moderate heat till brown on one side.
5 Turn and brown on other side.
6 Drain on absorbent paper and serve.

Jelly Roll

    5 eggs, separated
    ½ cup sugar
    2 tablespoons lemon juice
    1 tablespoon grated lemon rind
    ¼ teaspoon salt
    ¼ teaspoon cream of tartar
    1 cup cake flour, sifted
    confectioners' sugar
    8 oz apricot or other fruit jam

1 Beat egg yolks, add sugar and beat until creamy. Add lemon juice and rind.
2 Beat egg whites until stiff; add salt and cream of tartar.
3 Fold yolk mixture into whites.
4 Combine sifted flour with egg mixture.
5 Blend lightly.
6 Pour batter into a 10 inch x 15 inch jelly roll pan lined with wax paper.
7 Bake for 12-15 minutes in an oven pre-heated to 375°F.
8 Invert on a tray which has been sprinkled with confectioners' sugar.
9 Remove wax paper, fill with favourite jam filling and roll at once.
10 Sprinkle with confectioners' sugar.

Chicken Paprikash (see page 48)

LUNCHEON

Menu No. 2

Serves 8

Mamma's Chicken Soup

Liver Strudel
and/or
Baked Stuffed Eggplant

Spinach Salad

French-Fried Onions
and/or
Savory Rice

Apple Snow

Tutti Fruiti Bars

Coffee or Tea

Fruit Strudel (see page 46)

Mamma's Chicken Soup

1 x 6 lb chicken, quartered
½ bunch parsley
6 stalks celery with leaves
1 onion
6-8 carrots
1 ripe tomato
6 cups water
1 tablespoon salt
6 peppercorns

1 Place everything in a large (6 quart) covered pot.
2 Simmer for 3 hours over a low heat, stirring occasionally.
3 Strain.
4 Return carrots to the soup and serve. Use chicken in other dishes.

Liver Strudel

1¼ cups cake flour
⅓ cup shortening
cold water
2 onions
chicken fat for frying
8 chicken livers or ½ lb liver
4 hard-cooked eggs
¼ teaspoon salt
pepper
1 egg, beaten

1 Place flour on a pastry board and chop shortening into it, with a lifting and folding motion until well blended.
2 Add water to form soft dough, mixing with a cold knife or spoon. Chill.
3 Brown onions in chicken fat.
4 Add liver and fry until cooked.
5 Put liver and eggs through a grinder or food processor. Add the remaining fat from pan that livers were fried in.
6 Season with salt and pepper.
7 Roll out a small piece of dough at a time (about 4 inches x 12 inches).

8 Place liver mixture heaped up about 1 inch high across centre of strip of pastry.
9 Fold one side of pastry over liver. Paint with beaten egg.
10 Place other side over and paint again, sealing where pastry meets.
11 Press both ends together.
12 Bake in a hot oven for about 25 minutes or until cooked.
13 While hot, cut into 1½ inch lengths. Serve while warm with cocktails or as an entree.

Baked Stuffed Eggplant

2 large eggplants
3 cups stewed tomatoes
½ green pepper, chopped
4 tablespoons chopped onion
2 cups chopped meat
4 tablespoons margarine
2 cups fresh breadcrumbs
1 egg, beaten
1 teaspoon salt
dash pepper
dash paprika

Garnish
tomato halves
cauliflower flowerets

1 Cut eggplants in half lengthwise.
2 Scoop out the pulp; leave at least ¼ inch thick walls.
3 Submerge shells in cold water until ready for stuffing.
4 Drain shells and set aside.
5 Chop pulp from eggplant coarsely.
6 Combine pulp, tomatoes, green pepper, onion and meat. Sauté in margarine for 8 minutes. Remove from heat.
7 Add breadcrumbs and beaten egg.
8 Add salt, pepper and paprika to taste.
9 Mix ingredients well.
10 Stuff shells and sprinkle breadcrumbs on top.

11 Bake in a pre-heated oven at 350°F for 45 minutes.
12 Garnish with broiled tomato halves and floweretes of cauliflower.

Spinach Salad

2 lb fresh spinach
French Dressing
2 hard-cooked eggs

1 Wash spinach under cold water at least twice, subjecting each leaf to a flow of water. (Spinach is generally very sandy, so it is important to wash it most thoroughly to remove sand grains.)
2 Sit spinach in iced water for at least 15 minutes to crisp the leaves.
3 Clip the stems from each leaf.
4 Dry leaves in paper toweling to permit the dressing to coat the leaves.
5 Tear or snip leaves with scissors into bite-size pieces.
6 Add dressing and toss.
7 Finely chop egg or press through a sieve. Sprinkle over salad.
8 Serve on a chilled platter.

French-Fried Onions

3-4 large sweet Spanish onions
1 cup flour or thin fritter batter
salt

1 Peel onions.
2 Cut in ¼ inch slices and separate into rings.
3 Soak in a bowl of water in the refrigerator for several hours.
4 Drain and dip in flour or thin fritter batter.
5 Fry in deep fat at about 375°F.
6 Drain on brown paper and sprinkle with salt.

Savory Rice

¾ cup raw rice
2 tablespoons olive oil
1 tablespoon margarine
1 can tomatoes
1 clove garlic, crushed
1 onion, finely chopped
1½ tablespoons chopped green pepper
salt and pepper
2 cups boiling water

1 Wash rice very thoroughly then dry well.
2 Heat oil and margarine in a skillet.
3 Add rice and brown lightly.
4 Add the other ingredients and season with salt and pepper.
5 Add the boiling water, stir and simmer.
6 Stir occasionally and cook slowly until all liquid is absorbed.

Apple Snow

8 medium Greening or tart apples
½ cup water
6 egg whites
1½ cups sugar
2 tablespoons lemon juice
¼ cup almond slivers

1 Peel, core and slice apples.
2 Put apple slices and water in a saucepan; cover tightly and cook slowly until it becomes a mash.
3 Shake pan occasionally to prevent sticking.
4 Put mashed apples into a blender and blend for 5 seconds. Set aside.
5 Beat egg whites until they hold a peak.
6 Gradually beat in sugar and lemon juice until egg whites are quite stiff and smooth.
7 Fold into hot apple sauce and blend thoroughly.
8 Serve chilled with Tutti Fruiti Bars.

Tutti Fruiti Bars

¾ cup sifted enriched flour

1½ teaspoons baking powder

1 teaspoon salt

2 eggs

1 cup sifted confectioners' sugar

3 tablespoons melted shortening

1 cup chopped nuts

1 cup chopped dates

¾ cup chopped mixed candied fruit

1 Combine and sift flour, baking powder and salt.

2 Beat eggs until foamy, gradually beat in sugar.

3 Stir shortening into mixture.

4 Add sifted dry ingredients and blend thoroughly.

5 Mix in nuts, dates and candied fruit.

6 Spread in a well-greased 8 inch x 8 inch x 2 inch square pan.

7 Bake in pre-heated oven at 325°F for 35 minutes or until top has a crust.

LUNCHEON

Menu No.3

Serves 6

Mushroom and Barley Soup

Mock Cheese Blintzes
and/or
Stuffed Fillet of Sole

Eggplant Croquettes
and/or
String Beans French Style

Bread Pudding

Coffee or Tea

Mushroom and Barley Soup

1 medium-size onion
2 tablespoons butter
½ lb mushrooms, sliced
1 pint boiling water
1 carrot, diced
1 potato, diced
1 rib celery
¼ cup barley
1 teaspoon salt
dash pepper
¼ teaspoon sugar
1 pint milk

1 Fry onion in butter until yellow, add mushrooms and sauté for 10 minutes.
2 Add 1 pint water, carrots, potato, celery and barley.
3 Cook slowly for 1½ hours.
4 Add seasoning and milk and simmer for 10 minutes before serving.

Mock Cheese Blintzes

½ lb cream cheese
12 salted crackers
2 eggs, lightly beaten
4 tablespoons butter or margarine
2 tablespoons red currant jelly

1 Spread a layer of cream cheese between two salted crackers.
2 Dip into beaten egg and fry in hot butter.
3 Dot with red currant jelly.
4 Serve hot.

Stuffed Fillet of Sole

3 lb sole fillets
breadcrumbs, seasoned with salt, pepper and paprika

8 oz cooked whole mushrooms, chopped (leave some whole for sauce)
4 oz can mushrooms, stems and pieces
parsley, finely chopped
2 cans cream of mushroom soup
¾ cup white wine
Cheddar cheese, grated

1 Dip fish in seasoned breadcrumbs.
2 Combine chopped mushrooms and parsley.
3 Place about 2 tablespoons of this mixture on each slice of fish.
4 Roll up and fasten with toothpicks.
5 Place fish in a baking dish.
6 Combine soup and wine and pour over fish.
7 Sprinkle with grated cheese.
8 Add whole mushrooms to sauce.
9 Cover and bake in a pre-heated oven at 400°F for about 15 minutes.
10 Uncover and continue cooking for about 15 minutes until fish flakes.

Eggplant Croquettes

1 large eggplant
1 egg
¼ teaspoon garlic powder
¼ cup Romano cheese
½ teaspoon salt
½ teaspoon pepper
½ teaspoon nutmeg
½ teaspoon oregano
½ cup breadcrumbs

1 Cut eggplant into quarters.
2 Steam for 5 minutes. Remove peel and chop eggplant.
3 Add rest of ingredients, except breadcrumbs, and mix together well.
4 Shape into croquettes and roll in breadcrumbs.
5 Fry in oil at 450°F until golden brown.

String Beans French Style

2 packets frozen string beans
1 can mushroom soup
grated cheese

1 Cook and drain beans.
2 Add soup and mix well.
3 Top with grated cheese.
4 Bake in the oven at 350°F until hot and
  cheese melts.

Bread Pudding

1 quart milk
2 cups stale breadcrumbs
2 eggs
½ cup sugar
1 teaspoon vanilla
jelly or jam (optional)
sauce or custard (optional)

1 Heat the milk and pour it over the breadcrumbs. Allow them to soak until they
  are soft.
2 Beat the eggs, add the sugar and vanilla,
  and stir into the mixture of crumbs and
  milk.
3 Mix thoroughly, pour into a buttered
  baking dish, and bake in a moderate oven
  at 300°F for about 45 minutes.
4 If desired, jelly or jam may be served with
  the bread pudding, or any sauce, such as
  lemon or vanilla, or custard. The pudding
  may be served either hot or cold.

LUNCHEON

Menu

No.4

Serves 6-8

Cantaloupe Soup

Herring Salad
and/or
Stuffed Shoulder of Veal

Vegetable Salad
and/or
Pan-Fried Apples

Mushrooms with Wine

Fruit Strudel

Coffee or Tea

Cantaloupe Soup

1 large ripe cantaloupe
½ teaspoon cinnamon
2¼ cups orange juice
2 tablespoons lime juice
fresh mint sprigs

1 Remove seeds from melon and cube the pulp.
2 Place pulp and cinnamon in an electric blender and purée.
3 Combine orange and lime juice and stir into purée.
4 Chill.
5 Serve in chilled soup bowls garnished with mint.

Herring Salad

1 herring
2 hard-cooked eggs
1 raw onion
1 apple
4 walnuts
2 tablespoons vinegar
pepper to taste
sugar if desired

1 Soak herring overnight.
2 Remove skin and bones from herring.
3 Combine all ingredients except vinegar and combine in a food chopper.
4 Add vinegar, mix thoroughly.
5 Chill.
6 Serve on lettuce leaf.

Stuffed Shoulder of Veal

5-6 lb shoulder of veal

Stuffing
¼ cup chopped walnuts
¼ cup margarine
¾ cup chopped stewed prunes
3 cups soft breadcrumbs
1 tablespoon chopped parsley
½ teaspoon salt
dash freshly ground pepper
1 egg, lightly beaten

1 Ask the butcher to bone the shoulder of veal and slit a pocket for the stuffing.
2 In a large skillet sauté nuts in margarine until lightly browned.
3 Remove from heat and add remaining ingredients.
4 Stir and mix well.
5 Wipe the veal with a damp cloth and fill the cavity with nut-fruit stuffing.
6 Skewer or sew the cavity closed.
7 Lay veal on a rack in a roasting pan and cover.
8 Bake in a pre-heated oven at 325°F until cooked. (Allow about 20-25 minutes per pound.)
Note: Stuffing ingredients make about 5 cups of stuffing.

Vegetable Salad

Dressing
1 teaspoon salt
¼ teaspoon paprika
4 tablespoons lemon juice
⅔ cup olive oil

1 clove garlic
1 medium cucumber, peeled and thinly sliced
1 cup cooked beets, diced
1 cup artichoke hearts

1 Combine dressing ingredients and mix thoroughly in a bowl rubbed with a clove of garlic.
2 Mix vegetables and pour over dressing.
3 Stand for 1 hour.
4 Drain and serve on lettuce leaves.

Pan-Fried Apples

4-5 apples
5 tablespoons margarine
5 tablespoons sugar

1 Core, but do not peel, the apples.
2 Slice into pieces about $\frac{1}{4}$ inch thick or cut into wedge-shaped pieces about $\frac{1}{2}$ inch thick.
3 Melt margarine in a skillet.
4 When hot place apple slices or pieces in the pan and brown on one side. Turn and brown on other side. Sprinkle with sugar.
5 Remove from the pan and serve slices as a garnish, or serve wedges in a hot dish.

Mushrooms with Wine

$\frac{1}{2}$ lb mushrooms
3 tablespoons margarine
$\frac{1}{3}$ cup boiling water
$\frac{1}{2}$ teaspoon salt
$\frac{1}{8}$ teaspoon paprika
dash nutmeg
$\frac{1}{3}$ cup sauterne

1 Prepare mushrooms.
2 Cook covered with butter and boiling water for 12 minutes.
3 Add other ingredients.
4 Heat and serve.

Fruit Strudel

4 eggs
2 tablespoons butter or margarine, melted
2 cups flour
4 tablespoons butter or margarine
$\frac{1}{2}$ cup sugar
$\frac{1}{2}$ cup currants
$\frac{1}{2}$ teaspoon cinnamon
$\frac{1}{2}$ cup blanched, slivered almonds
$\frac{1}{2}$ cup chopped walnuts
2 cups mixed candied fruit
2 tablespoons melted butter
$\frac{1}{2}$ cup sugar
1 cup hot water
cinnamon
sugar

1 Beat eggs well.
2 Add 2 tablespoons melted butter or margarine.
3 Sift flour and add gradually.
4 Knead dough for 20 minutes.
5 Cut dough into 4 parts. Roll out each piece until paper thin.
6 To make filling, melt 4 tablespoons butter or margarine and brush over stretched dough.
7 Spread sugar, currants, cinnamon, nuts and fruit on the dough.
8 Roll up and brush with butter. Place in a well-greased pan.
9 Combine 2 tablespoons melted butter, sugar and water to make a syrup. Baste strudel.
10 Pre-heat oven to 400°F and bake strudel for 30 minutes.
11 Reduce heat to 350°F and bake for another 30 minutes.
12 Baste frequently with syrup.
13 Sprinkle strudel with cinnamon and sugar as soon as you remove it from the oven.
14 Serve either warm or cold.

LUNCHEON

No.5

Serves 6

Chicken Broth

Chopped Liver
and/or
Chicken Paprikash

California Salad Bowl

Asparagus Almondine
and/or
Tomato Aspic

Lady Fingers Lime Mold

Coffee or Tea

Chicken Broth

1 x 4 lb fowl
6 cups cold water
1 small carrot
2 stalks celery
½ bay leaf
¼ teaspoon peppercorns
1 onion sliced
salt and pepper

1 Put all the ingredients into a pot and heat gradually to boiling point.
2 Cook until meat is tender, cool, remove fat and strain.
3 Serve chicken broth hot and retain chicken for use on another occasion in salads or croquettes.

Chopped Liver

1 lb calves' liver or beef liver
2 raw onions, OR 4 cooked onions
2 hard-cooked eggs
chicken fat or margarine
salt and pepper

1 Broil liver for 2 minutes on each side, then boil for about 2 minutes.
2 Cut into pieces and put through food chopper with onions and eggs.
3 Add enough chicken fat to make a paste and mix well.
4 Season to taste.

Chicken Paprikash

3 lb broiling fowl
seasoned flour
chicken fat or margarine
1 medium-sized onion
1 small can tomatoes
1 small can button mushrooms, OR ¼ lb
   sliced fresh mushrooms

1 clove garlic, crushed (optional)
salt and pepper
dash paprika

1 Wash and dry fowl.
2 Coat with seasoned flour.
3 Heat a heavy skillet with a little chicken fat or margarine and brown chicken.
4 Cut onion into small pieces and brown in the fat after removing chicken.
5 Purée tomatoes.
6 Put in a covered pot, add chicken, browned onions, mushrooms, garlic, salt, pepper and paprika.
7 Simmer slowly over a low heat for about 2 hours or until tender.
8 Serve over boiled rice or with a rice ring. Extra gravy can be served at the table in a separate container.

Note: Chicken Paprikash can be cooked the day before and reheated.

California Salad Bowl

4 carrots, cut into strips
1 cucumber, sliced
1 bunch radishes
1 bunch celery
1 medium head celery-cabbage
5 medium tomatoes
1 head iceberg lettuce
4 medium stalks endive, sliced
1 green pepper, cut thinly
1 clove garlic
celery salt
salt and pepper
1 teaspoon diced capers
3 hard-cooked eggs, sliced

1 Prepare all greens several hours before using.
2 Use a fancy vegetable cutter to strip carrots and cucumber. Cut radishes into 'rosebuds'. Dice celery. Cut celery-cabbage into round slices about ¼ inch thick. Quarter tomatoes. Cut lettuce into shreds.
3 Rub salad bowl with garlic. Put all vegetables into another bowl. Season with

celery salt, pepper and salt. Shake and stir vegetables until mixture is evenly seasoned. Add capers and eggs.
4 Arrange bowl with salad in the center and garnish edge of bowl with alternate slices of tomato, endive stalks, strips of carrot and thin pieces of green pepper.
5 Serve with French, Russian or plain salad dressing.

Asparagus Almondine

2 cans green asparagus
2 oz margarine
¼ cup toasted almonds, slivered
2 teaspoons lemon juice

1 Heat asparagus and drain when ready to serve.
2 Melt margarine, stir in almonds and lemon juice.
3 Serve hot over heated asparagus.

Tomato Aspic

2 tablespoons gelatin
¼ cup cold water
½ cup boiling water
4 cups tomatoes, fresh or canned
1 tablespoon chopped onion
½ teaspoon celery seed
1 teaspoon salt
1 teaspoon sugar
2 teaspoons lemon juice
stuffed olives
sweet pickles, sliced
asparagus
carrots, finely shredded

1 Soften gelatin in cold water. Then dissolve it in boiling water.
2 Cook tomatoes, onion and seasonings for 15 minutes.
3 Strain.
4 Add lemon juice and dissolved gelatin.

5 Add olives, sweet pickles, asparagus and carrots.
6 Pour into a mold and chill.

Lady Fingers Lime Mold

2 packets lime gelatin
2 cups hot water
1 pint lime sherbet
1 cup cold water
1½ cups melon balls
1 packet lady fingers
fruit jam

1 Dissolve gelatin in hot water.
2 Add sherbet.
3 Add cold water.
4 Chill until partially set.
5 Add melon balls.
6 Pour into a mold and refrigerate for 24 hours to set.
7 Turn mold out onto a platter.
8 Coat 1 side of each of the lady fingers with a thin layer of fruit jam and stick onto outside of mold.

LUNCHEON

Menu

No. 6

Serves 6

Leek Soup

Mushroom Pie
and/or
Tuna Lasagna

Pear Macaroon Salad

Baked Zucchini with Tomatoes
and/or
Apple Squash Scallop

Apricot Soufflé

Coffee or Tea

Leek Soup

6-8 leeks
3 tablespoons butter
soup stock
salt and pepper
chopped parsley
croutons
grated cheese

1 Cut leeks into small pieces and cook for
  5-6 minutes in the butter, turning
  frequently so as not to brown.
2 Add 3-4 cups of soup stock and
  seasonings.
3 Cook for about 1 hour.
4 Strain and serve with croutons and
  cheese.

Mushroom Pie

2 pie crusts

Filling
3 eggs
1½ cups heavy cream, OR 1½ cups half
  milk/half cream
dash nutmeg
salt and pepper
¼-½ cup grated Swiss cheese
butter

Mushroom mixture
2 tablespoons chopped shallots, scallions
  or onions.
3 tablespoons butter
1 lb fresh mushrooms, sliced
salt
1 teaspoon lemon juice
2 tablespoons port, sherry or Madeira

1 Partially bake pie crusts at 400°F.
2 Beat filling ingredients together.
3 Cook shallots in butter until transparent.
4 Stir in filling mixture. Cover pan and
  cook for 8 minutes over a low heat.

5 Uncover and cook until liquid evaporates.
6 Add remaining mushroom mixture
  ingredients.
7 Fill crusts with filling.
8 Dot with butter.
9 Pre-heat oven to 375°F.
10 Bake in upper third of oven for 25-30
  minutes or until brown.

Tuna Lasagna

9 lasagna noodles
11 oz can tomato sauce
11 oz can marinara sauce
6 oz can tomato paste
2 bay leaves
2 x 7 oz cans tuna
8 oz packet mozzarella cheese, sliced
¼ cup grated Parmesan cheese
2 eggs
1¾ cups creamed cottage cheese

1 Cook noodles according to directions.
2 Mix sauces, paste and bay leaves in a
  saucepan and simmer for 10 minutes.
3 Remove bay leaves.
4 Drain tuna.
5 In a lightly greased 2-quart casserole or
  8 inch x 12 inch baking dish layer as
  follows: ⅓ of the noodles; ½ of the tomato
  sauce; ½ of the mozzarella cheese slices; all
  of the tuna; ½ of the Parmesan; ⅓ of the
  noodles.
6 Beat eggs until whites and yolks are just
  blended.
7 Fold in cottage cheese.
8 Spread all of it over the noodles.
9 Layer the remaining noodles, sauce and
  Parmesan.
10 Cut the remaining mozzarella into ½ inch
  strips and arrange on top of the lasagna.
11 Bake in a pre-heated oven at 350°F for 30
  minutes.
12 Stand for 10 minutes to set the layers.
13 Cut into squares and serve.

Pear Macaroon Salad

1 packet cream cheese, thinned with cream
1 can pear halves, drained
rolled macaroon crumbs
lettuce cups
maraschino cherries
mayonnaise

1 Spread a thin layer of cheese on half a pear.
2 Cover with another half pear and dip whole pear in crumbs.
3 Serve in deep cups of lettuce.
4 Garnish with a cherry.
5 Serve with additional mayonnaise.

Baked Zucchini with Tomatoes

1 teaspoon chopped onion
1 clove garlic (optional)
1 tablespoon olive oil
2½ cups tomatoes
2 lb zucchini
2 cups breadcrumbs
½ cup grated American cheese
salt and pepper

1 Brown onion and garlic in oil.
2 Remove garlic, add tomatoes.
3 Slice zucchini thinly and place in layers in a greased casserole. Alternate with tomatoes, breadcrumbs and cheese. Finish with a layer of breadcrumbs on top.
4 Season each layer of zucchini with salt and pepper.
5 Bake uncovered in a hot oven (400°F) for 1 hour.

Apple Squash Scallop

2 eggs, beaten
2 cups canned apple sauce
1 packet frozen squash, thawed

¼ cup butter, melted
½ cup evaporated milk
¼ cup brown sugar
dash nutmeg
½ teaspoon salt
1½ cups buttered breadcrumbs
½ cup toasted almonds
1 tablespoon butter

1 Put eggs in a bowl.
2 Add apple sauce, squash, butter, milk, sugar, nutmeg and salt. Mix thoroughly.
3 Pour into a shallow buttered baking pan about 8 inches x 8 inches.
4 Top with buttered breadcrumbs and sprinkle with almonds.
5 Bake in a pre-heated oven at 375°F for 25-30 minutes.

Apricot Soufflé

2 tablespoons butter or margarine
4 tablespoons flour
⅓ cup sugar
dash salt
1 cup scalded milk
3 eggs
½ teaspoon vanilla extract
1 can apricots, OR 3 cups fresh apricots and ¼ cup sugar

1 Melt the butter in a double boiler.
2 Add the flour, sugar and salt. Stir in the hot milk.
3 Bring this mixture to boiling point.
4 Separate the yolks and whites of the eggs.
5 Add egg yolks, stirring continually until mixture thickens; cool.
6 Stir in vanilla extract and apricots.

Apricot Soufflé (see page 52)

LUNCHEON

Menu

No.7

Serves 4

Minestrone

Sweet and Sour Salmon
and/or
Marinated Chicken

Cucumber and Pineapple Salad

Rice Pilaf
and/or
Fried Apples

Lady Fingers Chocolate Pudding

Coffee or Tea

Sweet and Sour Salmon (see page 56)

Minestrone

1½ quarts good beef stock, or 12 bouillon
   cubes
1 small cabbage, shredded
2 stalks celery
½ lb spinach, finely chopped
3 carrots, sliced
2 large tomatoes
2 peppercorns
1½ cups diced potatoes
1 lb fresh lima beans
1 clove garlic, finely chopped (optional)
2 sprigs parsley
1 large onion, sliced thinly
salt to taste

1 Heat stock to boiling point.
2 Add all the ingredients.
3 Bring to a boil again and simmer for 3
   hours.
4 Serve piping hot.

Sweet and Sour Salmon

1 stalk celery with leaves
parsley
1 medium onion, sliced
2 carrots, cut in slices
2 tablespoons vinegar
1½ lb salmon, sliced
⅓ cup brown sugar
6 ginger snaps
⅓ cup seedless raisins
juice of 1 lemon

Garnish
toasted almond slivers
lemon wedges
carrot rounds

1 Boil celery, parsley, onion and carrots in
   water for 15 minutes.
2 Add vinegar and salmon slices.
3 Reduce heat to simmer and poach salmon
   gently for 12 minutes until cooked (the
   liquid should cover the fish).

4 If fish becomes soft, add a little more
   vinegar.
5 Remove fish to a platter and keep warm.
6 Reserve liquid.
7 In another saucepan combine brown
   sugar, ginger snaps, raisins, lemon juice
   and enough hot liquid to dissolve sugar.
8 Stir and cook over low heat.
9 Add more liquid as needed to make a
   sauce of desired consistency.
10 Add more sugar or vinegar if desired to
    give sauce a definite sweet-sour taste.
11 Pour over fish.
12 Garnish with toasted almond slivers,
    lemon wedges and carrot rounds.

Marinated Chicken

2 x 2½-3 lb broiling chicken, cut into
   pieces
monosodium glutamate
garlic powder
1½ oz whiskey
¾ cup soy sauce
¾ cup water
2 teaspoons sugar

1 Sprinkle chicken with monosodium
   glutamate and garlic powder.
2 Combine the remaining ingredients and
   marinate chicken for 6 hours.
3 Brush chicken with marinade.
4 Barbecue chicken on grill or under broiler.

Cucumber and Pineapple
Salad

1 envelope or 1 tablespoon gelatin
¼ cup cold water
¼ cup sugar
¼ cup hot water

¼ teaspoon salt
⅔ cup pineapple syrup
1 tablespoon lemon juice
¼ cup mild vinegar
1 cup peeled, diced cucumber, drained
1 cup canned pineapple

1 Soak gelatin in ¼ cup cold water for 5 minutes.
2 Add sugar, salt and hot water.
3 Stir until dissolved.
4 Add pineapple syrup, lemon juice and vinegar.
5 Cool until mixture thickens.
6 Add cucumber and pineapple cut into small pieces and drain.
7 Turn into individual molds, rinse in cold water, and chill.
8 When firm, turn out mold onto lettuce.

Rice Pilaf

¼ cup chopped onion
4 tablespoons margarine
1½ cups uncooked rice
2½ cups boiling chicken broth
¼ teaspoon salt
⅛ teaspoon pepper

1 Pre-heat oven to 375°F.
2 Sauté onion in margarine in heavy casserole until tender and transparent, but not browned.
3 Add rice and stir over a low heat until rice grains turn golden.
4 Add chicken broth and season with salt and pepper.
5 Cover tightly and bake for 5 minutes.
6 Reduce the heat to 350°F and bake for 15-20 minutes or longer, until rice has absorbed all the stock.

Note: The onion and rice may be sautéed in the casserole ahead of time. Then, 25 minutes before serving time, add the boiling broth and continue the recipe.

Fried Apples

2 cans sliced pie apples, including juice
1 cup sugar
½ lemon, juice and rind
2 tablespoons butter
⅛ teaspoon salt

1 Put all ingredients into a skillet.
2 Cook over a medium heat until apples brown.
3 Serve with meat or poultry.

Lady Fingers Chocolate Pudding

2 squares chocolate
8 tablespoons confectioners' sugar
2 tablespoons water
4 eggs
1 teaspoon vanilla
½ lb lady fingers

1 Put the chocolate, sugar and water in a double boiler and heat, stirring constantly.
2 Separate the eggs and beat the yolks. Add yolks to the chocolate mixture and cook until thick. Set aside to cool.
3 Beat egg whites until stiff; fold into the mixture and add the vanilla.
4 Separate the lady fingers. Line a mold or baking dish with waxed paper and cover the sides and bottom with a layer of lady fingers.
5 Cover with the chocolate mixture, add another layer of lady fingers, and continue until all the mixture is used.
6 Use lady fingers on top to mark out the number of pieces to be cut. Set in the refrigerator for 24 hours.
7 To serve, remove from mold, pull off the waxed paper, and place on a flat dish.

Note: Since there is much more than needed, this dessert can be stored in the refrigerator for another meal.

LUNCHEON

No. 8

Serves 6

Clear Madrilene
with Knaidlach or Matzo Balls

Sweet and Sour Tongue
and/or
Barbequed Lamb Ribs

Cranberry Relish Mold

Kasha
and/or
Eggplant and Okra

Southern Ambrosia

Sponge Cookies

Coffee or Tea

Clear Madrilene

3 lb hip beef
2 lb beef bones (from the knee)
3 quarts water
salt
4 carrots
4 leeks
2 onions stuck with cloves
2 turnips
4 celery stalks
1 bay leaf
dash thyme
12 ripe tomatoes

1 Put the beef and bones in a large soup pot.
2 Add water and salt. Bring to the boil, skimming frequently.
3 Add all the other ingredients except the tomatoes.
4 Simmer for 3 hours.
5 Then add the tomatoes and cook for 1 hour longer.
6 Strain through a fine sieve until clear.

Knaidlach or Matzo Balls

2 eggs, separated
$\frac{3}{4}$ cup boiling water
1 cup matzo meal
1 teaspoon chicken fat
salt and pepper to taste

1 Beat egg whites until stiff.
2 Add water.
3 Mix in beaten yolks.
4 Add matzo meal, fat and seasonings.
5 Form into balls.
6 Chill for a few hours.
7 Cook for 20 minutes in boiling water or soup.

Sweet and Sour Tongue

1 smoked or pickled tongue
8 bay leaves
1 teaspoon pepper
1 teaspoon cloves

Sauce
6 ginger snaps
$\frac{1}{2}$ cup brown sugar
$\frac{1}{4}$ cup vinegar
1 lemon, sliced
1 cup soup stock, OR 3 bouillon cubes and 1 cup water
$\frac{1}{2}$ cup raisins
juice of 1 onion

1 Wash smoked tongue and soak overnight.
2 Cover with water and seasonings and cook slowly for 2-4 hours or until tender.
3 When cooked, remove from water and pull off skin.
4 Cut off root of tongue and slice into $\frac{1}{4}$ inch slices.
5 Mix sauce ingredients together and cook very slowly until smooth.
6 Additional sugar and vinegar may be added to give sauce a sharp flavor.
7 Add to sliced tongue. Serve very hot.

Barbequed Lamb Ribs

3-4 lb lamb ribs
1 cup boiling water
1 cup brown sugar
$\frac{1}{2}$ teaspoon ginger
salt and pepper
2 tablespoons soy sauce
1 teaspoon mustard
1 packet beef broth mix
$\frac{1}{2}$ teaspoon garlic salt

1 Combine all ingredients, except lamb, to make a marinade.
2 Marinate ribs 4-6 hours.
3 Bake for $2\frac{1}{2}$ hours in a pre-heated oven at 350°F.
4 Baste every $\frac{1}{2}$ hour.

Cranberry Relish Mold

2 cups fresh cranberries
rind and pulp of 1 orange
rind and pulp of 1 lemon
1 apple, peeled and cored
½ cup crushed pineapple, well drained
½ cup sugar
2 packets apple gelatin
2 cups cranberry juice
2 cups apple juice

1 Grind cranberries, orange, lemon and apple in a blender.
2 Add sugar.
3 Let mixture stand while preparing gelatin.
4 Prepare gelatin according to directions on box, using juices instead of water.
5 Add ground fruit.
6 Pour into a mold.
7 Chill till set.

Kasha

1½ cups kasha
1 egg
1 can onion soup, OR 1 packet onion
   soup, dehydrated
boiling water
1 can sliced mushrooms (optional)

1 Use casserole in which you intend to serve the kasha.
2 Mix kasha with unbeaten egg and dry in a 350°F oven for about 25 minutes, until grains separate, stirring occasionally.
3 Add onion soup.
4 Add boiling water to cover.
5 Add sliced mushrooms.
6 Cover and bake in a pre-heated oven at 350°F for 45-50 minutes.
7 Remove cover and bake for another 15 minutes.

Eggplant and Okra

1 eggplant, peeled and cubed
1 onion, chopped
3 tomatoes, quartered
12 okra pods, sliced
salt and pepper
1 tablespoon finely chopped parsley

1 Combine eggplant, onion, tomatoes, okra, salt and pepper.
2 Cook for 30 minutes.
3 Sprinkle with chopped parsley and serve.

Southern Ambrosia

4 medium sweet oranges
½ cup sugar
½ cup shredded coconut
1 can crushed pineapple

1 Peel oranges and cut across the grain into ⅛ inch slices.
2 Place layers of orange slices, sugar, coconut and crushed pineapple in a large bowl.
3 Place in the refrigerator overnight to set.

Sponge Cookies

1 cup flour
1 cup sugar
3 eggs
1 teaspoon vanilla

1 Mix sifted dry ingredients.
2 Add eggs and vanilla. Mix well.
3 Drop spoonfuls of mixture onto greased paper to form cookies.
4 Bake in a pre-heated oven at 350°-400°F until brown around edges.

LUNCHEON

Menu

No.9

Serves 8

Creole Gumbo

Salmon Pastry Roll
and/or
Lamb Curry

Roasted Pepper Salad

Stewed Rhubarb
and/or
Petit Peas with Mint

Stewed Dried Fruit

Springeles Cookies

Coffee or Tea

Creole Gumbo

1 chicken
6 large tomatoes
50 okra pods
2 tablespoons margarine
½ pod red pepper without seeds
1 onion, finely chopped
1 bay leaf
1 sprig parsley, finely chopped
1 sprig thyme, finely chopped
3 quarts chicken broth, OR 3 quarts hot
    water and 8 cubes chicken bouillon
salt
cayenne pepper to taste

1 Clean and cut up chicken.
2 Skin tomatoes and chop finely, reserving the juice.
3 Wash and stem okra and slice into ½ inch pieces.
4 Heat margarine. Add chicken and red pepper.
5 Cover and simmer for 10 minutes, then add onion, bay leaf, parsley, thyme and tomatoes, stirring frequently to prevent sticking.
6 Add okra and when ingredients are well browned, add juice from tomatoes.
7 Cook for 10 minutes longer, then add chicken broth or hot water and bouillon cubes, and salt and cayenne pepper to taste.
8 Simmer gently for 1 hour.

Salmon Pastry Roll

½ cup finely cut celery
½ cup finely cut green pepper
2 tablespoons margarine, melted
2 cups flaked salmon
¼ teaspoon salt
½ teaspoon pepper
2 cups pie pastry

1 Cook celery and green pepper in margarine until tender.

2 Add flaked salmon and season to taste.
3 Roll out pastry ¼ inch thick. Spread with salmon filling and roll up.
4 Place on a baking sheet and bake at 400°F for 30 minutes.
5 Slice and serve hot with mushroom sauce.

Lamb Curry

3 lb lamb, shoulder or neck, cubed
¼ cup flour
2 garlic cloves, minced
4 large onions, sliced
¾ cup margarine
4 small apples, pared and chopped
4 tablespoons curry powder
4 tablespoons brown sugar
4 tablespoons raisins
2 tablespoons Worcestershire sauce
2 lemons, sliced
4 tablespoons shredded coconut
¾ cup chopped walnuts
½ teaspoon grated lime peel
1 tablespoon salt
2 cups water

1 Roll lamb in flour.
2 Sauté garlic and onions in margarine in a large skillet for 5 minutes.
3 Add meat and sauté for 10 minutes, stirring constantly.
4 Add apples and curry powder.
5 Simmer for 5 minutes, stirring occasionally.
6 Add remaining ingredients.
7 Bring to the boil, reduce heat, cover and simmer for 1 hour.
8 Serve with shredded coconut and chutney.

Roasted Pepper Salad

1 jar roasted sweet red peppers
2 small cans flat anchovies, finely diced
1 onion, finely chopped
wine vinegar

1 Combine ingredients.
2 Marinate overnight in wine vinegar.
3 Serve spoonfuls on individual lettuce beds.

Stewed Rhubarb

2 cups sugar
½ cup water
2 lb rhubarb
lemon peel strips (optional)

1 Mix the sugar and water in a saucepan and bring to the boil.
2 Wash the stems of the rhubarb and cut into 1 inch lengths.
3 Add rhubarb to syrup and cook until it is tender enough to be pierced with a fork.
4 If desired, lemon peel may be added.
5 Put into a serving dish and allow to cool.

Petit Peas with Mint

2 lb peas
boiling water
⅛ teaspoon salt
4 tablespoons margarine
⅛ teaspoon sugar
2 teaspoons finely chopped fresh mint

1 Drop peas into boiling, salted water. (Use as little water as possible.)
2 Cook for about 15-20 minutes, or until peas are tender. Drain well and add all other ingredients.
3 Mix well by shaking.
4 Serve at once.

Stewed Dried Fruit

1 lb mixed dried fruit
2 cups cold water
½ cup sugar

2 tablespoons lemon or orange rind
3 tablespoons candied ginger, cut into small pieces

1 Wash and rinse fruit very carefully in cold water.
2 Put into saucepan and add 2 cups cold water.
3 Cook at a moderate heat until fruit is tender.
4 Remove fruit from liquid and add sugar, lemon or orange rind and candied ginger.
5 Bring to the boil and reduce to a light syrup. Pour over fruit and serve.
Note: Fruit may also be baked in a pre-heated oven at 325°F for about 45 to 60 minutes.

Springerle Cookies

4½ cups sifted cake flour
1 teaspoon baking powder
1 teaspoon salt
4 eggs, beaten
1 lb confectioners' sugar
1 tablespoon lemon rind
2 tablespoons anise seeds

1 Combine and sift flour, baking powder and salt.
2 Mix eggs, sugar and lemon rind thoroughly.
3 Add sifted dry ingredients and mix well.
4 Roll dough on a floured board to ½-¾ inch thickness.
5 Cut with cookie cutter or knife.
6 Design may be pressed in with a Springerle rolling pin and cut apart.
7 Sprinkle anise seeds on greased baking sheet.
8 Arrange cookies on sheet.
9 Allow to stand exposed to air for 12 hours.
10 Bake in a pre-heated oven at 350°F for 30 minutes.
11 Store in a covered crock or jar for 2-3 weeks to season.

LUNCHEON

No.10

Serves 8

Chilled Fruit Soup

Vegetarian Chopped Liver
and/or
Epicurean Fillets of Sole

Avocado Mold

Baked Potatoes and Onions
and/or
Creamed String Bean Casserole

Wiener Nusstorte

Coffee or Tea

Chilled Fruit Soup

1 cup orange juice
¾ cup grapefruit juice
5 cloves
2 inch piece of cinnamon
1 cup pineapple juice
1 tablespoon cornstarch
⅓ cup cold water
¼ cup sugar
⅛ teaspoon salt

1 Combine orange and grapefruit juice, cloves and cinnamon.
2 Stand for several hours or overnight in a cool place.
3 Heat pineapple juice to boiling point.
4 Add cornstarch mixed with cold water.
5 Cook for 3 minutes. Add sugar, salt and fruit juices.
6 Place in the refrigerator to chill and serve very cold.

Vegetarian Chopped Liver

3 medium onions, diced
1 lb cooked fresh or canned string beans
3 hard-cooked eggs, chopped
⅛ teaspoon salt
⅛ teaspoon pepper
1 tablespoon mayonnaise

1 Fry onions until they are translucent.
2 Drain string beans and chop.
3 Add hard-cooked eggs, onions and seasonings.
4 Serve on a lettuce leaf.

Epicurean Fillets of Sole

3 lb fish fillets
flour
margarine or butter
1½ lb green grapes

1½ pints sour cream
salt and pepper
1 teaspoon paprika

Stuffing
12 tablespoons breadcrumbs
1 lb fresh mushrooms, chopped and sautéed in margarine
9 tablespoons finely chopped parsley
3 hard-cooked eggs, finely chopped
3 raw eggs
1½ teaspoons salt
1 teaspoon pepper
1½ teaspoons monosodium glutamate

Garnish
lemon slices
parsley sprigs

1 Mix stuffing ingredients thoroughly.
2 Press about 3 tablespoons stuffing onto each fillet.
3 Roll up and secure with toothpicks.
4 Dredge the rolls with flour and sauté on all sides in butter or margarine over a low heat until lightly browned. Transfer rolled stuffed fillets to a baking pan or casserole.
5 Put green grapes in skillet and cook for 1 minute.
6 Add 1½ pints sour cream.
7 Remove from heat and season with salt, pepper and paprika.
8 Spoon sauce into casserole over fish and bake uncovered in a pre-heated oven at 300°F for 35-45 minutes.
9 Serve on a platter and garnish with lemon parsley and grapes.

Avocado Mold

2 cups boiling water
2 packets lemon or lime gelatin
2 cups sour cream
2 cups mayonnaise
2 cups mashed avocado, OR 2 large avocados, mashed

1 Pour boiling water over gelatin and stir until dissolved.
2 Cool.
3 Add sour cream, mayonnaise and avocado.
4 Mix well.
5 Rinse ring mold in cold water.
6 Pour mixture into wet mold.
7 Chill thoroughly.
8 Unmold on lettuce and serve with Chantilly Dressing.

Baked Potatoes and Onions

2 cups Zwieback crumbs
6 medium potatoes, peeled and thinly sliced
2 large onions, thinly sliced
1-2 tablespoons chopped parsley
1 teaspoon salt
¼ teaspoon ground black pepper
½ cup grated Parmesan cheese
1½ cups sour cream
2 tablespoons Parmesan cheese (extra)

1 Line a well-buttered casserole dish (2 quarts or larger) with 1 cup Zwieback crumbs.
2 Combine sliced potatoes, onions and parsley in the casserole. Sprinkle with salt and pepper.
3 Mix ½ cup grated Parmesan cheese with sour cream, and spoon over the vegetables.
4 Top with remaining cup of crumbs mixed with two tablespoons Parmesan cheese.
5 Place dish in a pre-heated oven, cover and bake at 375°F for 45 minutes or until potatoes are tender when pierced with a fork.

Creamed String Bean Casserole

2 lb frozen French-style string beans
1 can water chestnuts
½ cup slivered almonds
1 can cream of asparagus soup
1 can French-fried onions

1 Cook and drain string beans.
2 Add water chestnuts, slivered almonds, soup and ½ can French-fried onions.
3 Bake in a pre-heated oven at 275°F for 20 minutes.
4 Sprinkle remaining French-fried onions on top a few minutes before serving.

Wiener Nusstorte

1 cup sugar
6 eggs, separated
2 cups ground nuts

Garnish
fresh cream
grated chocolate

1 Beat sugar and egg yolks for 20 minutes.
2 Add ground nuts and well-beaten egg whites.
3 Pour batter into 2 buttered spring form cake tins and bake in a moderate oven until mixture no longer sticks to the sides of the tin.
4 Cover with cream and garnish with chocolate or nuts or any tart jam.

LUNCHEON

No. 11

Serves 6

Lentil Soup

Sweetbread Casserole
and/or
Yom Tov Pot Roast
with Potato Pudding

Scalloped Eggplant
and/or
Sautéed Mushrooms

Baked Prune Whip

Coffee or Tea

Lentil Soup

2 cups lentils
3 quarts cold water
meat bones
2 lb meat
1 cup diced carrots
½ cup diced celery
1 small onion
1 cup tomato soup
2 frankfurters, thinly sliced
salt and pepper

1 Wash and soak lentils for several hours or overnight.
2 Place lentils in a pot with cold water, meat bones and meat. Boil steadily for 3 hours or until meat is tender.
3 Remove meat and skim fat off top of liquid.
4 Add vegetables and soup. Cook until tender.
5 Ten minutes before serving drop in sliced frankfurters.
6 Season and serve.

Sweetbread Casserole

2 pairs sweetbreads
salt
lemon juice
1 large onion, chopped
¼ lb mushrooms
2 tablespoons flour
1 cup cooking liquid
2 tablespoons tomato paste
peas
carrot cubes
potato balls

Garnish
chopped parsley

1 Soak sweetbreads in salted cold water for about 30 minutes.
2 Plunge into boiling water to which salt and lemon juice have been added.

3 Simmer for about 15 minutes.
4 Remove sweetbreads and plunge into cold water. Retain cooking liquid.
5 Remove membrane and skin.
6 Cut into bite-size pieces and sauté in butter.
7 Sauté onion and mushrooms.
8 Add flour to pan and make a paste, using 1 cup of cooking liquid and tomato paste.
9 Serve in a casserole with cooked peas, carrot cubes and potato balls.
10 Sprinkle with chopped parsley and serve.

Yom Tov Pot Roast

4 lb brisket
1 teaspoon salt
¼ teaspoon pepper
¼ teaspoon garlic powder
1 cup Concord grape wine
1 medium carrot, finely chopped
1 large onion, finely chopped
1 lb jar fruit compote
1 large apple, peeled, cored and sliced
1 teaspoon cinnamon
½ teaspoon ginger
2 tablespoons potato starch

1 Brown meat in a Dutch oven (add a little oil if necessary).
2 Add salt, pepper, garlic powder, wine, carrot, onion and liquid from jar of compote.
3 Bring to the boil.
4 Reduce heat, cover and simmer 2½ hours, or until tender.
5 Add fruits, cinnamon and ginger.
6 Cook for 15 minutes.
7 Remove meat and fruit to a warm platter.
8 Skim fat from pan juices and discard.
9 Mix potato starch with cold water.
10 Stir into pan juices and cook until thickened.
11 Pour pan juices over meat and fruit and serve.

Potato Pudding

4 tablespoons margarine
1 onion, chopped
7 raw potatoes, grated
3 well-beaten eggs
2 tablespoons butter

1 Heat 2 tablespoons margarine and cook onion.
2 Add potatoes and mix well.
3 Add beaten eggs.
4 Melt 2 tablespoons margarine in a baking pan.
5 Pour in potato mixture and bake at 350°F for 1½ hours.

Scalloped Eggplant

1 eggplant, peeled and cubed
½ onion, finely chopped
2 tablespoons margarine
¾ tablespoon finely chopped parsley
½ cup margarined crumbs

1 Cook eggplant in small amount of water with piece of lemon added to keep it from discoloring.
2 Cook until soft, not mushy.
3 Cook onion in margarine until yellow.
4 Add parsley and eggplant.
5 Put in margarined baking dish.
6 Cover with margarined crumbs.
7 Bake in pre-heated oven at 375°F until crumbs are brown.

Sautéed Mushrooms

½ lb mushrooms, broken in pieces
flour for dredging
3 tablespoons margarine
few drops onion juice
paprika

¼ teaspoon salt
⅓ cup hot water or broth
1 teaspoon finely chopped parsley
dry toast

1 Dredge mushrooms with flour.
2 Melt margarine in heavy frying pan.
3 Add everything except water and toast and cook for 5 minutes.
4 Add water and cook for 4 minutes longer.
5 Sprinkle with parsley and serve on toast.

Baked Prune Whip

⅔ cup stewed prunes
½ cup sugar
5 egg whites
½ tablespoon lemon juice

Garnish
custard
kumquats

1 Rub prunes through strainer or purée in a blender.
2 Add sugar and cook for 5 minutes. Set aside to cool.
3 Beat egg whites until stiff.
4 Add prune mixture and lemon juice.
5 Pile lightly into a margarined baking dish and bake for 30 minutes in a slow oven at 300°F. Serve hot or cold with custard and garnished with kumquats.

LUNCHEON

Menu

No. 12

Serves 8

Russian Borscht

Chopped Herring
and/or
Sweet and Sour Meat
with Dumplings

Jellied Avocado Salad

Baked Cabbage
and/or
Glazed Carrots

Fresh Fruit Cup

Wine Cake

Coffee or Tea

Weiner Nusstorte (see page 66)

Russian Borscht

3 lb beef shinbone
2 lb beef brisket, cubed
2 quarts water
2 cups diced fresh beets
4 cups shredded cabbage
2 large onions, chopped
3½ cups canned tomatoes
¾ cup lemon juice
6 garlic cloves, minced
¼ cup chopped parsley
1 small bay leaf, crumbled
1 teaspoon paprika
3 tablespoons sugar
1 teaspoon salt
freshly ground black pepper

1 Cover shinbone and brisket with water.
2 Bring to the boil, reduce heat, cover and simmer for 1 hour.
3 Add vegetables, lemon juice and seasonings and simmer for 2 hours.
4 Remove shinbone.
5 Trim off meat and discard bone.
6 Cut meat into 1 inch pieces.
7 Return meat to soup and simmer for 10 minutes before serving.

Chopped Herring

2 medium milch herring
½ cup white vinegar
2 medium green apples
2 hard-cooked eggs
⅛ teaspoon pepper
¼ cup water
2 medium onions
2 slices white bread
2 tablespoons sugar

Garnish
1 egg yolk, finely chopped

Yom Tov Pot Roast (see page 68)

1 Put all ingredients through a food chopper or chop finely.
2 Serve on lettuce and garnish with egg yolk.

Sweet and Sour Meat with Dumplings

2 lb boneless chuck, cut into individual servings
1 medium onion, sliced
¾ cup vinegar
½ cup brown sugar
paprika
few whole allspice berries
⅛ teaspoon salt
⅛ teaspoon pepper
¼ teaspoon paprika
water to cover
1 packet dumpling mix, OR your favorite dumpling recipe

1 Combine all ingredients in a large pot and cover with water.
2 Simmer until tender.
3 Put into a 12 inch uncovered casserole. Make dumplings and drop on top.
4 Bake at 350°F until browned.

Jellied Avocado Salad

1 packet lemon flavoured gelatin
1 cup boiling water
2 tablespoons lemon juice
2 tablespoons pineapple juice
1 large avocado
¼ cup blanched almonds, shredded
8 slices pineapple
8 crisp lettuce leaves
mayonnaise

1 Dissolve gelatin in boiling water, stirring until dissolved.
2 When cooled, add lemon and pineapple juice.

3 Peel and cut avocado into cubes and arrange in molds with shredded almonds.
4 When gelatin is beginning to set, pour into molds and set aside and chill.
5 Place slice of pineapple on crisp lettuce and arrange mold on pineapple. Serve with mayonnaise.

Baked Cabbage

1 medium onion
1 tablespoon margarine
2 tablespoons flour
2 cups water
½ teaspoon Worcestershire sauce
¼ teaspoon salt
⅛ teaspoon pepper
dash paprika
1 small cabbage
2 tablespoons breadcrumbs
2 tablespoons margarine

1 Peel and slice onion; fry to a light brown in 1 tablespoon margarine.
2 Add flour, water and seasonings.
3 Shred cabbage into a saucepan.
4 Pour mixture over cabbage.
5 Cook slowly for about 1 hour.
6 Pour mixture into a baking dish.
7 Sprinkle top with breadcrumbs.
8 Dot with remaining margarine.
9 Bake in a pre-heated oven at 450°F until breadcrumbs turn brown. Serve.

Glazed Carrots

2 lb fresh carrots
2 tablespoons margarine
3 tablespoons brown sugar

1 Peel carrots.
2 Place in iced water for 15 minutes.
3 Cut each carrot into 2 inch lengths.
4 Boil carrots in water until tender.
5 Place boiled carrots in a baking dish and lay flat.

6 Melt margarine and spread over carrots.
7 Sprinkle with brown sugar.
8 Brown in a pre-heated oven at 350°F until carrots are brown.
9 Spoon sauce over carrots and serve.

Fresh Fruit Cup

½ pineapple
3 oranges
3 bananas
1 cup strawberries
2 tablespoons boiling water
1 tablespoon sugar
2 tablespoons Cointreau, Kirsch, or other liqueur

Garnish
8 half slices lemon
8 pitted black cherries

1 Peel and dice pineapple, oranges and bananas.
2 Wash and hull strawberries.
3 Mix all fruits together.
4 Dissolve sugar in boiling water and add.
5 Add liqueur.
6 Chill thoroughly in refrigerator.
7 Garnish with lemon slices and pitted cherries.

Wine Cake

12 eggs, separated
1 cup sugar
1 cup cake meal
1 cup wine
1 cup finely chopped walnuts
½ teaspoon salt

1 Mix egg yolks and sugar.
2 Add rest of ingredients and fold in stiffly beaten whites.
3 Spoon into a greased 10 inch tube pan.
4 Bake for 1 hour at 325°F.
5 Invert on a wire rack and cool before removing.

LUNCHEON

Menu No.13

Serves 8-10

Mushroom-Wine Soup

Liver Strudel
and/or
Baked Glazed Corned Beef

Potato Salad

Hot Carrots in Mint Sauce
and/or
Smothered Peas

Pareve Ice Cream

Lemon Wafers

Coffee or Tea

Mushroom-Wine Soup

⅓ cup oil
1 cup coarsely chopped onion
1 cup or 2 oz dried mushrooms, OR 1 lb fresh mushrooms
½ cup chopped celery
1 clove garlic, chopped
2 bay leaves
pepper to taste
1 sprig parsley
2 quarts beef broth
¾ teaspoon monosodium glutamate
¾ teaspoon Worcestershire sauce
1 cup sauterne or sweet white wine

1 Heat oil in a heavy saucepan.
2 Add onions, mushrooms, celery, garlic, bay leaves, pepper and parsley.
3 Cook for about 10 minutes over a moderate heat until onions and celery are well browned.
4 Slowly add broth, monosodium glutamate and Worcestershire sauce.
5 Bring to the boil, reduce heat, and simmer covered about 50 minutes.
6 Cool slightly.
7 Pour one ladle of soup at a time into blender.
8 Turn blender on and keep adding soup until all soup has been puréed.
9 Add wine, adjust seasonings to taste and serve.

Liver Strudel

1 large onion, chopped
¼ green pepper, chopped
1 stalk celery, chopped
2 tablespoons chicken fat
½ lb calves liver
2 eggs, hard-cooked
salt and pepper
rich pastry dough

1 Chop all ingredients except dough and eggs and brown in a frying pan.
2 Add eggs and put mixture through a meat grinder.
3 Cool and season to taste.
4 Roll out dough very thinly, cut into 3 inch squares and place a small amount of mixture on each square.
5 Roll up or make envelopes.
6 Chill, then bake for 20 minutes in a pre-heated oven at 450°F.

Baked Glazed Corned Beef

8 lb boneless corned brisket or pickled beef
30 cloves
8 slices pineapple
maraschino cherries

Glaze
1½ cups brown sugar
2 teaspoons cornstarch
1 teaspoon powdered mustard
2 tablespoons molasses
2 teaspoons lemon juice
¼ cup pineapple juice
grated orange and lemon rind

1 Boil beef until just underdone.
2 Place flat on a pan lined with aluminium foil.
3 Trim surplus fat off beef. Decorate with cloves, pineapple and cherries (hold on with toothpicks until glazed).
4 Combine glaze ingredients and cook over a low heat, stirring until thickened. Pour glaze over meat.
5 Bake in the oven at 300°F for 45 minutes.
6 Baste with glaze drippings.
7 If you wish to serve meat later, completely cover with aluminium foil and return to oven at 200°F for 30 minutes. Meat can be kept longer covered in a warm oven with the heat off.
Note: Cooked beef can be kept undecorated in

the freezer with its cooking liquid in a separate container. Reheat and decorate when required.

Potato Salad

3 tablespoons olive oil
1 tablespoon wine vinegar
salt and pepper to taste
2 cups cooked, cubed warm potatoes
2 hard-cooked eggs, chopped
1 cup minced celery
1 tablespoon minced shallots
3 tablespoons minced parsley
1 tablespoon prepared mustard
$\frac{1}{3}$ cup mayonnaise

1 Combine oil, vinegar, salt and pepper.
2 Pour over warm potatoes.
3 Toss lightly and chill.
4 Add remaining ingredients.
5 Toss again.

Hot Carrots in Mint Sauce

$1\frac{1}{2}$ cups diced carrots
2 tablespoons butter
1 teaspoon cornstarch
1 tablespoon sugar
$\frac{1}{3}$ cup water
1 tablespoon shredded mint leaves
few drops lemon juice
grated rind of $\frac{1}{3}$ lemon

1 Cook diced carrots in small quantity of slightly salted water.
2 Drain and push carrots to one side of pan. Add butter and melt over a low heat.
3 Blend cornstarch with sugar, add water, mint leaves, lemon juice and rind.
4 Add this to the butter and cook. Mix in the carrots as the sauce cooks.

Smothered Peas

$\frac{1}{4}$ onion
1 tablespoon margarine
1 packet frozen peas
1 small lettuce
$\frac{1}{8}$ teaspoon salt
$\frac{1}{8}$ teaspoon pepper

1 Chop onion and sauté in margarine for a few minutes, but do not brown.
2 Add peas, either thawed or frozen.
3 Tear up the lettuce into pieces and cover peas with it. (Add no water.)
4 Cook slowly in a covered pan for about 15 minutes, or until peas are tender. Season with salt and pepper and serve.

Pareve Ice Cream

1 carton pareve Dessert Whip
2 eggs, separated
10 oz packet frozen strawberries or other fruit OR $\frac{1}{2}$ cup chocolate syrup, OR $\frac{1}{2}$ cup sugar and 3 oz semi-sweet chocolate

1 Whip the Dessert Whip.
2 Add egg yolks and strawberries or chocolate.
3 Beat egg whites (with sugar if using semi-sweet chocolate).
4 Mix together and freeze.
5 Defrost 20-30 minutes before serving.
6 Serve with lemon wafers.

Lemon Wafers

$2\frac{1}{2}$ cups sifted enriched flour
$\frac{1}{2}$ teaspoon baking powder
$\frac{1}{8}$ teaspoon salt
1 cup margarine
$\frac{3}{4}$ cup sugar
1 egg
2 tablespoons lemon juice
1 teaspoon grated lemon rind

1 Combine and sift flour, baking powder and salt.
2 Cream margarine.
3 Add sugar gradually and cream thoroughly.
4 Blend in egg, lemon juice and rind.
5 Add sifted dry ingredients.
6 Mix well.
7 Chill dough for 1 hour.
8 Force through a cookie press onto an ungreased baking sheet.
9 Bake in a pre-heated oven at 400°F for 10-12 minutes.

LUNCHEON

No. 14

Serves 8-10

Southern Bisque

Cheese Quicks
and/or
Tante Bessie's Fish in Shells

Roquefort Cheese Ring

Sautéed Green Tomatoes
and/or
Rice and Parsley

Pound Cake

Coffee or Tea

Southern Bisque

2 cans tomato soup
$\frac{1}{4}$ teaspoon baking soda
2 cups milk
2 cans creamed corn
4 tablespoons butter
$\frac{1}{8}$ teaspoon salt
$\frac{1}{8}$ teaspoon pepper

1 Heat tomato soup.
2 Add soda, milk and creamed corn.
3 Cook over a moderate heat for 15 minutes.
4 Add butter, salt and pepper.
5 Cook for 20 minutes.
6 Serve hot.

Cheese Quicks

1 cup prepared biscuit mix
1 cup grated cheese
$\frac{1}{4}$ teaspoon salt
$\frac{1}{2}$ cup water

1 Combine biscuit mix, cheese and salt.
2 Stir in water.
3 Put mixture through a cookie press, using small shapes.
4 Bake on an ungreased sheet (tray) in a pre-heated oven at 450°F for about 10 minutes.
Note: This recipe yields 24 Cheese Quicks.

Tante Bessie's Fish in Shells

3 lb halibut
2 cups milk
1 onion, diced
green pepper, diced
1 can tuna fish
1 can salmon
4 slices white bread

$\frac{1}{2}$ cup catsup
2 oz butter
salt and pepper to taste
breadcrumbs
paprika

1 Cook halibut with milk, onion and green pepper.
2 Cool; bone and skin fish.
3 Drain tuna and salmon and crumble into the cooked halibut.
4 Soak bread in soup from the halibut.
5 Add catsup, salt, pepper and soaked bread to the fish mixture.
6 Put mixture into greased shells.
7 Top with melted butter, breadcrumbs and paprika.
8 Bake in a pre-heated oven at 350°F until hot and browned.

Roquefort Cheese Ring

1 tablespoon gelatin
$\frac{1}{4}$ cup cold water
1 cup hot tomato soup
$\frac{1}{2}$ cup Roquefort cheese
1 packet cream cheese
$\frac{1}{2}$ cup mayonnaise
$\frac{1}{2}$ teaspoon Worcestershire sauce
1 teaspoon grated onion
1 tablespoon vinegar
$\frac{1}{2}$ cup diced celery

1 Soak the gelatin in cold water, then dissolve in hot soup.
2 Cool.
3 Add mashed cheese, mayonnaise and remaining ingredients.
4 Pour into an oiled ring mold and chill until firm.

Sautéed Green Tomatoes

4 medium green tomatoes
3 tablespoons margarine or butter

1 Slice tomatoes thinly.
2 In a skillet melt margarine or butter and
   sauté slices of green tomato.
3 Do not let slices get mushy.
4 Serve hot.

Rice and Parsley

1 cup rice
4 cups boiling, salted water
2 cups rich milk or cream
4 eggs, lightly beaten
$\frac{1}{3}$ cup melted butter or margarine
1 cup grated cheese
2 cups chopped parsley
1 onion, grated
$\frac{1}{4}$ teaspoon salt
$\frac{1}{8}$ teaspoon pepper

1 Cook rice in water for about 15-20
   minutes or until tender.
2 Drain and rinse with hot water.
3 Drain thoroughly again to allow rice to
   fluff.
4 Mix rice with all other ingredients.
5 Pour in a well buttered spring mold and
   bake in a pre-heated oven at 375°F for
   about $\frac{1}{2}$ hour.

Pound Cake

$2\frac{1}{4}$ cups cake flour
$\frac{1}{2}$ teaspoon salt
1 cup margarine
1 cup sugar
5 eggs, separated
1 teaspoon brandy

1 Sift flour and salt.
2 Cream margarine.
3 Add sugar slowly and continue beating
   until it is light and fluffy.
4 Add egg yolks until mixture is thick and
   lemon colored.

5 Add brandy and beat thoroughly.
6 Beat egg whites until stiff but not dry.
7 Gently fold beaten egg whites into
   mixture.
8 Gradually fold in dry ingredients until
   mixture is smooth.
9 Pour into a greased loaf pan.
10 Bake in a pre-heated oven at 300°F for
   about $1\frac{1}{4}$-$1\frac{1}{2}$ hours.

LUNCHEON

No.15

Serves 6

Rice Soup

Vegetable Liver
and/or
Chicken in a Blanket

Avocado Salad

Stuffed Squash
and/or
Savory Beans

Fruit Mold

Aizenblauzen

Coffee or Tea

Rice Soup

½ cup uncooked rice
½ teaspoon salt
½ cup canned chick peas
2 quarts water
½ can tomato sauce
⅛ teaspoon pepper
lemon wedges

1 Add rice, salt and chick peas to water and boil gently for about 1½ hours.
2 Add tomato sauce and pepper, and simmer for 15 minutes.
3 Serve with lemon wedges.

Vegetable Liver

1 onion, finely sliced
2 tablespoons margarine
1 cup cooked string beans
2 hard-cooked eggs
3 strips celery
1 small green pepper

Garnish
tomato wedges

1 Brown onion in margarine.
2 Finely chop all ingredients and combine.
3 Chill.
4 Serve on a lettuce leaf.
5 Garnish with tomato wedges.

Chicken in a Blanket

½ cup catsup
½ cup vinegar
3 tablespoons margarine
3 tablespoons brown sugar
1 clove garlic, crushed
1 teaspoon salt
1 teaspoon dry mustard
1 teaspoon chili powder
¼ teaspoon cayenne pepper

dash Tabasco sauce
2 onions, sliced
2 x 3 lb chickens, cut into serving pieces

1 Mix the ingredients, except onion and chicken, in a large saucepan.
2 Bring to the boil and allow to cool.
3 Preheat oven to 375°F.
4 Add sliced onion and chicken to the sauce.
5 Cut 6 pieces of aluminum foil 14 inches x 18 inches and grease one side of each with margarine.
6 Divide mixture evenly. Place on foil and wrap securely.
7 Place on baking sheet and bake for 1 hour.
8 Serve in foil.

Avocado Salad

3 medium avocados
½ teaspoon nutmeg
1 tablespoon sugar
3 tablespoons Kirsch

1 Peel avocados and cut the pulp into small cubes.
2 Sprinkle with nutmeg and sugar, and moisten with Kirsch.
3 Serve chilled on lettuce leaves.

Stuffed Squash

4 small yellow squash
½ onion, chopped
4 tablespoons margarine
¼ teaspoon salt
⅛ teaspoon pepper
2 eggs, well beaten
6 tablespoons breadcrumbs

1 Wash squash and cut in half lengthwise.
2 With a melon baller scrape out seeds and pulp, but do not break shells; leave ½ inch wall. Set pulp aside.

3 Sauté onion until lightly browned in 2 tablespoons margarine.
4 Add scraped-out squash and cook for about 15 minutes or until tender.
5 Remove from heat. Add salt and pepper.
6 Add well-beaten eggs and breadcrumbs.
7 Put into squash shells. Top with bread-crumbs and dot with remaining margarine.
8 Bake in a pre-heated oven at 350°F for about 30 minutes or until brown.

Note: Small eggplants can be substituted for squash.

Savory Beans

1½ cups beans
1 cup tomatoes
1 cup chicken broth
2 pimientos, finely diced
1 onion, finely chopped
1 clove garlic, finely chopped
¼ cup margarine
2 teaspoons salt

1 Soak beans overnight in cold water, drain and parboil until soft.
2 Put in a bean pot or baking dish.
3 Add other ingredients.
4 Cover and cook in a slow oven until beans have absorbed nearly all the sauce.

Fruit Mold

¼ oz unflavored gelatin
¼ cup cold water
½ cup boiling water
½ cup sugar
½ cup pineapple juice
½ cup orange juice
¼ cup lemon juice
2 slices pineapple
2 oranges
1 banana
6 walnuts

1 Moisten gelatin in cold water and dissolve in boiling water.
2 Add sugar and pineapple, orange and lemon juice. Allow to cool.
3 Dice the pineapple.
4 Peel oranges, remove the pulp from the sections, and cut it into small pieces.
5 Slice or dice the banana and break each nut into 6 or 8 pieces.
6 Mix the fruits and nuts, place in a mold that had been moistened with cold water, and pour the cold gelatin over them.
7 Allow this to solidify, turn from the mold and serve.

Aizenblauzen

2 eggs
1 cup flour
½ teaspoon salt
confectioners' sugar
cinnamon
1 cup peanut oil

1 Combine eggs, flour and salt. Work to a soft dough.
2 Roll to ⅛ inch in thickness on lightly floured board.
3 Cut into 3 inch strips to make 20 pieces.
4 Drop into hot oil and fry until golden brown.
5 Drain on brown paper and while hot sprinkle with confectioners' sugar and cinnamon.

LUNCHEON

Menu No.16

Serves 6-8

Gazpacho

Quiche Lorraine
and/or
Fried Smelts
with Tartar Sauce

Unique Potato Salad

Tomato Aspic
and/or
Carrots á la Jeanne

Apricot Rolls

Coffee or Tea

Gazpacho

1 cup finely chopped peeled tomatoes
½ cup finely chopped green pepper
½ cup finely chopped celery
½ cup finely chopped cucumber
¼ cup finely chopped onion
2 teaspoons finely chopped parsley
1 garlic clove, minced
3 tablespoons wine vinegar
2 tablespoons olive oil
1 teaspoon salt
¼ teaspoon freshly ground pepper
½ teaspoon basil
½ teaspoon Worcestershire sauce
2 cups tomato juice, OR 2 cups juice from
    can of tomatoes
½ cup chicken broth, chilled

Garnish
croutons

1 Combine all ingredients.
2 Cover and chill thoroughly in the
refrigerator for at least 4 hours.
3 Serve in chilled cups.
4 Top with croutons.

Quiche Lorraine

pastry for 9 inch pie plate
1 tablespoon margarine or butter
1 onion, thinly sliced
1 cup Gruyére or Swiss cheese, cubed
¼ cup grated Parmesan cheese
4 eggs, lightly beaten
2 cups cream, OR 1 cup milk and 1 cup
    cream
¼ teaspoon nutmeg
½ teaspoon salt
¼ teaspoon white pepper

1 Preheat oven to 450°F.
2 Line a 9 inch pie plate with pastry and
bake for 5 minutes.

3 Heat margarine or butter and cook onion
until transparent.
4 Sprinkle onion and cheeses over the inside
of the partly baked pastry.
5 Combine eggs, cream, nutmeg, salt and
pepper and strain over the onion-cheese
mixture.
6 Bake the pie for 15 minutes.
7 Reduce oven temperature to 350°F and
bake for about 10 minutes or until a knife
inserted 1 inch from pastry edge comes out
clean.
Note: Quiche Lorraine may be frozen and
reheated while still frozen for 35-40 minutes.

Fried Smelts

2 lb smelts
2 cups oil or shortening
2 tablespoons corn oil margarine
2 eggs, lightly beaten
1½ cups breadcrumbs
⅛ teaspoon salt
⅛ teaspoon pepper

Garnish
lemon wedges
1 cup tartar sauce

1 Wash fish under cold water.
2 You may either remove heads or tails,
or just the heads, or leave both on.
3 With a sharp knife slit underside and
remove gut. Rinse fish.
4 Heat oil and add margarine for flavor. Do
not let it smoke.
5 Dip cleaned smelts in lightly beaten eggs,
drain.
6 Roll in seasoned breadcrumbs.
7 Fry fish on both sides in heated oil.
8 When breadcrumbs are lightly browned,
remove fish and place on several layers of
paper toweling to drain oil and promote
drying.
9 Serve with lemon wedges and tartar
sauce.

Tartar Sauce

¾ cup mayonnaise
3 tablespoons chopped pickle
2 tablespoons chopped capers
1 tablespoon finely chopped chervil
1 tablespoon finely chopped onion
1 teaspoon white horseradish

1 Combine all ingredients.
2 Blend them well.
3 Serve as garnish sauce with fried smelts.

Unique Potato Salad

6 large potatoes
3 tablespoons melted margarine, or goose
   or chicken fat
2 hard-cooked eggs
1 Bermuda onion, cubed
⅛ teaspoon salt
⅛ teaspoon pepper
finely chopped parsley
finely chopped green pepper
dash thyme
vinegar
2 teaspoons prepared mustard
3 egg yolks, beaten

1 Boil, peel and cube potatoes.
2 Pour 3 tablespoons melted butter or fat
   over hot potatoes. Add a few slices of
   hard-cooked egg and some onion.
3 Add salt, pepper, parsley, green pepper
   and thyme.
4 Boil enough vinegar to almost cover the
   salad.
5 Add prepared mustard to hot vinegar and
   pour onto the beaten egg yolks a little at a
   time.
6 Pour this dressing over the salad, chill
   thoroughly and serve.

Tomato Aspic

1 packet lemon gelatin
2 cups hot tomato juice
2 tablespoons vinegar
2 teaspoons Worcestershire sauce
½ cup chopped celery
1 cup chopped cucumber
1 onion, finely chopped
salt and pepper to taste

1 Dissolve gelatin in hot tomato juice.
2 When gelatin mixture begins to thicken
   add other ingredients.
3 Pour into a large mold or individual
   molds.

Carrots á la Jeanne

½ cup margarine
4 cups carrots, cut into thin strips
⅛ teaspoon salt
⅛ teaspoon freshly ground pepper

1 Melt margarine in a heavy frying pan.
2 Add carrots and turn until well coated.
3 Cover and cook over a very low heat until
   carrots are tender and slightly browned.
4 Just before carrots are cooked, sprinkle
   with salt and pepper.

Apricot Rolls

3 tablespoons shortening
1 cup sugar
3 eggs
3 cups flour
3 teaspoons baking powder
rind and juice of 1 orange
rind and juice of 1 lemon
½ lb stewed apricots, mashed
lemon icing (optional)

1 Cream shortening and sugar.
2 Add eggs, one at a time, and mix thoroughly.
3 Add flour, baking powder, fruit juices and rind.
4 Flour board well and divide dough into 3 parts. Take one part, add more flour if necessary, and pat with hand into an oval shape.

5 Place $\frac{1}{3}$ apricot in center. Fold over and place on a cookie sheet.
6 Do the same with the other two parts of dough.
7 Bake in a pre-heated oven at 350°F for 25 minutes.
8 When cool, cover with thin lemon icing if desired. Cut into $\frac{1}{2}$ inch slices.

Fried Smelts (see page 86)

LUNCHEON

Menu

No.17

Serves 6

Cream of Mushroom Soup

Eggplant Casserole
and/or
Halibut Salad

Fruit Salad

Baked Mushrooms
and/or
Spinach au Gratin

Caramel Custard

Coffee or Tea

Halibut Salad (see page 92)

Cream of Mushroom Soup

½ lb mushrooms
4 cups chicken stock
1 slice onion
¼ cup butter
¼ cup flour
¼ cup milk
¼ cup cream
¼ teaspoon salt
⅛ teaspoon pepper
lemon juice or grated nutmeg

1 Chop mushrooms. Add to stock with onion and cook for 20 minutes. Rub through a sieve or purée in a blender.
2 Reheat and bind with butter and flour cooked together.
3 Add milk and cream.
4 Reheat and season to taste.

Eggplant Casserole

1 large eggplant, diced
1 can cream of mushroom soup
⅓ can milk
½ cup onion, chopped
¾ cup prepared bread stuffing
1 egg, lightly beaten
1 cup shredded sharp Cheddar cheese
2 tablespoons breadcrumbs
2 tablespoons Parmesan cheese

1 Parboil eggplant in water for 15 minutes.
2 Mix soup with ⅓ can milk.
3 Add onion, stuffing, egg and cheese.
4 Mix with eggplant and put in a buttered casserole.
5 Sprinkle breadcrumbs and Parmesan cheese on top.
6 Bake, uncovered, for 45 minutes in a preheated oven at 350°F.

Halibut Salad

2 carrots
1 large onion
¼ teaspoon salt
⅛ teaspoon freshly ground pepper
⅛ teaspoon garlic powder
1-2 lb slice of halibut
1 tablespoon mayonnaise
½ teaspoon catsup
1 tablespoon lemon juice
1 stalk celery, diced

1 Pare carrots and slice thinly diagonally across the grain.
2 Peel onion and slice into rings ⅛ inch thick.
3 Place 1½ inches of water in a saucepan.
4 Add salt, pepper, garlic powder, carrots and onions.
5 Cook over a medium heat for about 45 minutes or until carrots and onions are soft.
6 Put fish into saucepan, add more water to cover and cook for about 20 minutes.
7 Allow to cool, and drain off water.
8 Flake fish in a bowl.
9 Add mayonnaise, catsup and lemon juice and blend.
10 Garnish the fish salad with onions, carrots and diced celery.
11 Serve on a bed of crisp lettuce.

Fruit Salad

2 eggs
¼ cup sugar
¼ teaspoon salt
3 tablespoons lemon juice
1 cup cream
fresh or canned fruit
marshmallows

1 Beat eggs well.
2 Add sugar and beat well.
3 Add salt and lemon juice.

4 Cook in the top of a double boiler until it has the consistency of boiled custard.
5 Cool and add whipped cream.
6 Add a generous amount of fruit such as apples, oranges, grapes or pineapple.
7 Add cubed marshmallows.
8 Place in the refrigerator for 24 hours.
9 Serve chilled.

Caramel Custard

2 tablespoons sugar
3 cups milk
3 eggs
$\frac{1}{8}$ teaspoon salt
$\frac{1}{4}$ cup sugar
1 teaspoon vanilla extract
$\frac{1}{8}$ teaspoon nutmeg

1 Caramelize 2 tablespoons sugar.
2 Scald the milk.
3 Dissolve caramelized sugar in milk.
4 Beat eggs lightly.
5 Add salt, sugar, vanilla and nutmeg.
6 Combine all ingredients with scalded milk.
7 Pour into 6 custard cups.
8 Set in a pan of hot water and bake in a pre-heated oven at 325°F for 30 minutes.
9 To test if cooked, insert a knife blade in the center of one of the puddings. When cooked it should come out clean.

Baked Mushrooms

2 lb large fresh mushrooms
2 teaspoons salt
$\frac{1}{8}$ teaspoon pepper
4 tablespoons butter
8 tablespoons cream

1 Wash mushrooms and place in a casserole.
2 Season with salt and pepper.
3 Dot with butter and add cream.
4 Cover and bake in a pre-heated oven at 350°F for about 30 minutes or until tender.

Spinach au Gratin

1 x 10 oz packet whole leaf spinach
1 clove garlic
1 cup tomato sauce or undiluted tomato soup
$\frac{1}{2}$ cup Parmesan cheese

1 Cook spinach as directed on packet.
2 Drain, if necessary.
3 Place in a shallow baking dish which has been well rubbed with a cut clove of garlic.
4 Cover with the tomato sauce or soup and sprinkle with grated cheese.
5 Cook in a pre-heated oven at 350°F until dish is bubbly and cheese is delicately browned.

LUNCHEON

Menu
No. 18

Serves 6

Mushroom and Barley Soup

Herring Ring
and/or
**Braised Duckling
with Glazed Oranges**

Jellied Spring Salad

Cabbage Hollandaise
and/or
Florida Asparagus

Coconut Meringue Cake

Coffee or Tea

Mushroom and Barley Soup

3 onions
2 leeks
1 parsnip
1 turnip
6 stalks celery
4 carrots
2 quarts water
2 lb short ribs
1 tablespoon salt
½ teaspoon pepper
½ cup medium barley
1 lb fresh mushrooms, OR 3 oz dried
    mushrooms

1 Clean and cut vegetables.
2 Put all vegetables except mushrooms in a pot with water, short ribs, salt and pepper.
3 Cook for about 1½ hours or until meat is tender.
4 Strain.
5 Allow to cool and skim off fat.
6 Soak barley while stock is cooking.
7 Add barley and sliced mushrooms to stock.
8 Cook for about 1½ hours until barley is soft and soup is thick.

Herring Ring

1 jar stuffed olives
1 tablespoon oil
1 large jar Bismark herrings
1 large can tuna fish
¼ lb margarine
1 teaspoon grated onion
1 teaspoon lemon juice

1 Place a border of olives in the bottom of an oiled ring mold.
2 Grind herring with the fish and remaining olives.

3 Cream the margarine and add onion and lemon juice.
4 Combine with the fish and mix well.
5 Pack mixture into the ring mold and place in the refrigerator to set firm.
6 Invert on a lettuce leaf and surround with quartered tomatoes or garnish with egg and caviar. Serve with Thousand Island Dressing. (See page 25.)

Braised Duckling with Glazed Oranges

1 x 5-6 lb duck
salt and pepper
1 cup orange juice
1 cup consommé
½ cup seedless raisins
1 cup currant jelly
1-2 tablespoons flour
2 large oranges
½ cup sugar
3 tablespoons water
1 tablespoon corn syrup

1 Cut duck into portions, wash and dry.
2 Brown thoroughly in a hot Dutch oven.
3 Season with salt and pepper and add orange juice, consommé and raisins.
4 Cover and cook in a pre-heated oven at 300°F for 2 hours.
5 Remove duck to a hot platter.
6 Skim off as much fat as possible from gravy.
7 Add currant jelly and when melted thicken with flour mixed to a thin paste in a little water. Use 1 tablespoon flour for each cup of gravy.
8 Peel and section oranges.
9 Combine sugar, water and corn syrup.
10 Bring to the boil.
11 Add orange sections and simmer for 5 minutes.
12 Pour sauce over duck and garnish with glazed oranges.

Jellied Spring Salad

1 packet lemon flavored gelatin
juice of 1 lemon
2 cups hot water
1 bunch spring onions, sliced
1 cucumber, diced
1 stalk celery, finely cut
1½ tablespoons mayonnaise

1 Mix gelatin, lemon juice and hot water.
2 Cool.
3 Beat in mayonnaise.
4 Add onions, cucumber and celery.
5 Serve with mayonnaise.

Cabbage Hollandaise

1 medium cabbage
1 tablespoon salt
3 egg yolks
juice of 1 lemon
⅛ teaspoon salt
⅛ teaspoon pepper
1 tablespoon margarine
1 tablespoon cold water
4 tablespoons margarine

1 Cut cabbage into six equal sections.
2 With a sharp knife trim out the hard
center and discard.
3 Boil sections in salted water for about
8-10 minutes or until cabbage is tender.
4 In the top of a double boiler, over water
that is **not** boiling, beat egg yolks.
5 Add lemon juice, salt, pepper, 1 tablespoon margarine and cold water.
6 Continue mixing until sauce becomes
firm.
7 Add 4 tablespoons melted margarine
gradually.
8 Spoon Hollandaise Sauce over cabbage
and serve.

Florida Asparagus

1 bunch of asparagus
grated peel of 1 orange
2 tablespoons margarine

1 Trim, wash and cook asparagus in a little
salted water until just tender. Drain
asparagus.
2 Mix orange peel and melted butter.
3 Pour over asparagus and serve.

Coconut Meringue Cake

¼ lb margarine
½ cup sugar
1 tablespoon vanilla
3 tablespoons orange juice
4 egg yolks
1 cup flour
1 teaspoon baking powder
¼ teaspoon salt
4 egg whites
¼ cup sugar
2 cups shredded coconut
cherry preserves

1 Cream margarine and sugar.
2 Add vanilla, orange juice and egg yolks.
Beat well.
3 Add sifted flour, baking powder and salt.
4 Spread batter thinly in 2 well-greased,
9-inch layer pans.
5 Beat egg whites until stiff. Gradually add
¼ cup sugar. Fold in coconut and spread
meringue over batter in pans.
6 Bake for 35 minutes in a pre-heated oven
at 350°F.
7 Spread a layer of strawberry jelly or jam
over one of the cakes. Place other cake on
top.
8 Decorate with cherry preserves and
coconut.
Note: Coconut Meringue Cake can also be
baked in a square pan and served without
garnishes.

LUNCHEON

Menu

No.19

Serves 8

Clear Soup

Baimel Herring
and/or
Sweet and Sour Tongue

Bing Cherry Mold

French-Fried Cauliflower
and/or
Carrot Ring Supreme

Hungarian Apple Cake

Coffee or Tea

Clear Soup

2-3 beef bones
3-4 cups water
2 onions
6 or 7 celery stalks
5 carrots
2 cubes beef bouillon
1 can tomatoes
⅛ teaspoon salt
⅛ teaspoon pepper
sugar to taste
1 tablespoon finely chopped parsley

1 Put beef bones and water in a large saucepan.
2 Trim ends off onions and add.
3 Break celery into 3-4 inch pieces and add.
4 Clean and scrape carrots, cut lengthwise and add.
5 Drop in bouillon cubes.
6 Cook over medium heat for 1 hour.
7 Add tomatoes.
8 Add salt, pepper and sugar.
9 Cook for 2-3 hours.
10 Strain through a fine sieve.
11 Serve with chopped parsley sprinkled on top.

Baimel Herring

2 dozen herrings
caraway seeds
2 bay leaves
mustard seeds
tiny hot peppers
1 cup olive oil

1 Soak and clean herring and remove heads. Place a layer on the bottom of a stone crock.
2 Sprinkle with some caraway seeds, bay leaves, mustard seeds and peppers.
3 Alternate layers of herring and spices.
4 Pour olive oil into crock until contents are covered.

5 Put a flat dish over top and weight this to keep herring pressed down firmly.
6 Stand for 3-4 weeks or until required. Serve as an entrée or appetizer.

Sweet and Sour Tongue

1 x 5-7 lb smoked or pickled tongue
8 bay leaves
1 teaspoon freshly ground pepper
1 teaspoon cloves

Sauce
6 ginger snaps
½ cup brown sugar
¼ cup vinegar
1 lemon, sliced
1 cup soup stock, OR 3 bouillon cubes dissolved in 1 cup hot water
½ cup seedless raisins
juice of 1 onion

1 Wash tongue and soak in water overnight.
2 Place tongue in pot and cover with water.
3 Add seasonings.
4 Cook slowly for 2-4 hours until tender.
5 Drain tongue and peel off skin.
6 Cut away root of tongue and discard.
7 Slice diagonally into ¼ inch pieces.
8 Mix sauce ingredients together.
9 Cook very slowly, stirring frequently, until smooth.
10 Additional sugar and vinegar may be added to sharpen flavor.
11 Pour hot sauce over sliced tongue and serve.

Bing Cherry Mold

1 can bing cherries
nuts
2 cups orange juice
1½ cups sherry
1 cup sugar
3 tablespoons gelatin

1 Drain cherries and reserve juice.
2 Stuff cherries with nuts and place in a mold.
3 Mix the juice from the cherries with 1½ cups orange juice, sherry and sugar.
4 Bring to the boil.
5 Soak gelatin in remaining orange juice and dissolve in the hot fruit syrup.
6 When mixture begins to set, pour into the mold over the cherries.
7 Stand aside to set, then serve.

French-Fried Cauliflower

1 fresh head cauliflower
2 eggs, beaten
2 tablespoons flour
pinch salt
½ cup oil or shortening

1 Cut cauliflower into small pieces and soak in salted water. Drain.
2 Boil in salted water for about 10 minutes or until tender. (Do not overcook or it will fall apart when handled.) Drain.
3 Dip cauliflower pieces in beaten egg. Roll in flour and salt.
4 Fry in oil or shortening to a golden brown, and serve plain or with Hollandaise sauce.

Carrot Ring Supreme

3 cups cooked, mashed carrot
2 tablespoons margarine
⅛ teaspoon salt
⅛ teaspoon freshly ground pepper
finely chopped parsley, chives or marjoram
1 tablespoon margarine
1 cup cooked peas

1 Combine mashed carrot with margarine, salt, pepper and herbs.
2 Grease ring mold with 1 tablespoon margarine. Add mixture.

3 Set in a pan of water and bake in a pre-heated oven at 400°F for 30 minutes.
4 Remove and stand aside for 10 minutes.
5 Unmold onto a platter, fill center with peas and serve.

Hungarian Apple Cake

3 cups flour
1 cup margarine
3 hard-cooked egg yolks
¾ cup sugar
¼ cup apple juice
1 egg (raw)
3 lb apples
sugar to taste
¼ cup raisins
¼ lb finely chopped almonds
1 egg white

1 Sift flour. Add margarine, egg yolks and sugar. Blend well.
2 Add apple juice and raw egg.
3 Knead dough for about 5 minutes.
4 Separate dough into 2 equal parts.
5 Roll out one part of dough until ¼ inch thick and place in a greased oblong baking pan.
6 Pare and thinly slice apples.
7 Place apples on top of dough. Sprinkle with sugar to taste. Add raisins.
8 Roll out remaining dough and cover mixture.
9 Brush with egg white and sprinkle with sweetened chopped almonds.
10 Bake in a pre-heated oven at 400°F for 10 minutes.
11 Reduce heat to 350°F and bake for 30 minutes longer.

LUNCHEON

No.20

Serves 8

Tomato Soup

Egg Anchovy Canapés
and/or
Casserole of Beef Tongue

Asparagus and Watercress Salad
with French Dressing

Oven-Fried Potatoes
and/or
Spanish Beans

Frosted Mandarin Orange Mold

Coffee or Tea

Tomato Soup

2-3 lb short ribs
1 onion, finely cut
1 tablespoon margarine
2 large cans tomatoes
¼ cup uncooked rice
⅛ teaspoon salt
⅛ teaspoon freshly ground pepper
sugar to taste

1 Place ribs in a pot and cover with water.
2 Boil for one hour.
3 Skim to remove scum.
4 Sauté onion in margarine and add to the meat.
5 Add tomatoes and cook for another hour.
6 Strain. Add rice, salt, pepper and sugar to strained liquid.
7 Cook until rice is soft and serve.

Egg Anchovy Canapés

8 lettuce leaves
8 pieces Holland rusk
1 tube anchovy paste
8 slices tomato
4 eggs, hard-cooked
½ cup Russian Dressing

1 Wash and dry lettuce leaves.
2 On each leaf place a round Holland rusk.
3 Spread a thin layer of anchovy paste on rusk.
4 Put slice of tomato on anchovy.
5 Place ½ egg (cut lengthwise) with cut side down on tomato.
6 Garnish with Russian dressing.

Casserole of Beef Tongue

1 x 5 lb beef tongue
2 onions
2 carrots
3 stalks celery with leaves
6 sprigs parsley
water to cover
1-2 tablespoons oil or shortening

Sauce
2½ tablespoons margarine, melted
2 slices onion
1 green pepper, chopped
1 small clove garlic
2½ cups tomatoes
1 bay leaf
1 teaspoon salt (optional)
6 peppercorns
½ teaspoon paprika
1 tablespoon chopped mushrooms
brown sugar to taste
2 teaspoons flour

1 Combine tongue, vegetables, parsley, water and oil and cook for 3 hours.
2 Drain and skin tongue.
3 Slice tongue into small pieces and put into a greased casserole.
4 Mix sauce ingredients together and spoon over the tongue.
5 Bake covered in a pre-heated oven at 350°F for 30 minutes.

Note: 3 tablespoons of chopped olives, capers or slivered almonds may be added to the sauce.

Asparagus and Watercress Salad

½ bunch cooked asparagus
¼ cup French Dressing
1 bunch watercress
1 teaspoon finely chopped chives

1 Marinate asparagus in French dressing for one hour.
2 Serve on a bed of watercress and sprinkle with chives.

French Dressing

4 thin slices onion
5 tablespoons vinegar
2 teaspoons sugar
2½ teaspoons salt
½ teaspoon paprika
dash cayenne pepper
1 cup olive oil

1 Stand onions in vinegar 30 minutes; strain.
2 Add sugar, salt, paprika and cayenne pepper and mix well.
3 Add oil and shake in a tightly covered container or beat until thick and smooth.
4 Chill.
5 Shake again before pouring over salad.

Oven-Fried Potatoes

8 potatoes, peeled
1 quart cold water
4 tablespoons margarine, melted
¼ teaspoon salt
⅛ teaspoon freshly ground pepper
½ teaspoon caraway seeds (optional)

1 Cut potatoes lengthwise into eight pieces.
2 Soak for 1 hour in cold water.
3 Dry well.
4 Dip in melted margarine and bake in a pre-heated oven at 400°F until delicately brown.
5 Turn occasionally while cooking.
6 Sprinkle with salt, pepper and caraway seeds before serving.

Spanish Beans

3 cups red beans
1 onion, chopped
2 celery stalks
1 teaspoon celery salt
½ teaspoon poultry seasoning
3 tablespoons margarine
1 tablespoon flour
dash paprika
salt
dash chili sauce
1 tablespoon catsup

1 Soak beans overnight, drain off water and wash.
2 Chop onion and add to the beans.
3 Put in a pot and add long stalks of celery.
4 Simmer for 3½ hours.
5 Add other ingredients and continue cooking for 30-45 minutes longer.
6 Remove celery stalks and serve.

Frosted Mandarin Orange Mold

3 packets orange gelatin
3 cups boiling water
1 pint orange sherbet
11 oz can mandarin orange sections with juice
15 oz can crushed pineapple with juice

1 Dissolve gelatin in boiling water.
2 Add other ingredients and mix.
3 Pour into a 3 quart mold and refrigerate overnight.
4 Garnish with additional mandarin sections.

LUNCHEON

Menu

No. 21

Serves 8

Potato Soup

Sardine-Stuffed Eggs
and/or
Stuffed Cabbage

Plain Cherry Ring

Broccoli with Almond Sauce
and/or
Peas and Onion

Linzer Torte

Coffee or Tea

Potato Soup

   2-3 small potatoes
   1 small onion, chopped
   3 tablespoons margarine
   1 tablespoon flour
   cooking liquid from potatoes
   soup stock
   dash cayenne pepper
   $\frac{1}{4}$ teaspoon salt
   $\frac{1}{8}$ teaspoon pepper
   1 tablespoon chopped parsley

1 Boil potatoes. Drain and retain cooking liquid. Mash potatoes.
2 Brown onion in margarine; add the flour and brown also.
3 Add the potato liquid and as much stock as you need.
4 Add seasonings and parsley.
5 Serve with croutons.

Sardine-Stuffed Eggs

   8 hard-cooked eggs
   1 tin skinned and boned sardines
   $\frac{1}{4}$ cup finely chopped parsley
   1 small onion, finely chopped
   1 teaspoon mayonnaise

1 Slice eggs in half lengthwise and remove yolks.
2 Blend egg yolks with remaining ingredients to form a smooth paste.
3 Stuff yolk mixture into halved egg whites.
4 Serve on lettuce leaf.

Stuffed Cabbage

   14-16 large cabbage leaves
   1 matzo, broken
   $\frac{1}{2}$ cup water
   1 lb ground beef
   1 egg, beaten
   1 large onion, diced
   $\frac{1}{4}$ cup lemon juice
   $\frac{1}{2}$ cup brown sugar
   $\frac{1}{4}$ cup water
   1 can tomato-mushroom sauce

1 Trim spines from cabbage leaves to make leaves flexible.
2 Place in a large pot of boiling water and simmer for 5 minutes.
3 Drain.
4 Soak broken matzo in $\frac{1}{2}$ cup water until soft.
5 Combine this mixture with meat and egg.
6 Place a heaped tablespoon of meat mixture in the center of each cabbage leaf.
7 Fold in the sides to cover meat and roll.
8 Shred some of the remaining raw cabbage and place in the bottom of a large saucepan.
9 Place cabbage rolls on top with open sides down.
10 Combine remaining ingredients and pour over cabbage rolls.
11 Bring to the boil and then reduce heat.
12 Simmer for about 1 hour, basting occasionally.

Plain Cherry Ring

   1 packet cherry gelatin
   1 cup boiling water
   1 cup juice from canned cherries
   2 tablespoons lemon juice
   1 can pitted bing cherries
   1 teaspoon oil to grease mold

1 Dissolve gelatin in water.
2 Add cherry juice and lemon juice and cool.
3 When cold add the drained cherries.
4 Put in a greased mold and chill.

Broccoli with Almond Sauce

   1 bunch fresh broccoli
   1 cup water

½ teaspoon salt
½ cup margarine, melted
¼ cup almonds, finely chopped

1 Wash broccoli thoroughly and cut off tough ends of stems.
2 Boil broccoli rapidly in salted water in uncovered pot.
3 Drain, pour over margarine and sprinkle with almonds before serving.
Note: Broccoli can also be served with Hollandaise sauce or plain melted margarine.

Peas and Onion

3 lb peas
½ cup water
2 tablespoons margarine
juice of ½ small onion OR 1 sliced onion cooked in margarine
⅛ teaspoon of salt
⅛ teaspoon of sugar

1 Cook peas in water and margarine, adding onion juice at the beginning of the cooking period.
2 If you prefer to use onion slices, cook separately and add after peas are drained.
3 Add salt and pepper and serve.
Note: Tiny pickled onions or thinly sliced green onions can also be substituted.

Linzer Torte

½ lb margarine
½ lb sugar
½ lb almonds, ground
3 eggs (keep one egg yolk for brushing top)
1 teaspoon cloves
1 teaspoon ground cinnamon
grated rind of 1 lemon
juice of 1 lemon
½ lb matzo meal
blackberry preserve

1 Mix all ingredients together except blackberry preserve.
2 Spread mixture with your hands over the bottom, and half way up the sides of a buttered springform tin.
3 Retain enough dough to make a lattice covering.
4 Fill shell with blackberry preserve (or any other preserve that you may prefer).
5 Make a lattice cross-patch with remaining dough across the top.
6 Brush egg yolk across top of torte.
7 Pre-heat oven to 350°F and bake torte for 45-50 minutes.

LUNCHEON

Menu

No. 22

Serves 4

Clear Tomato Soup

Stuffed Mushroom Caps
and/or
Chicken with Fried Rice

Bing Cherry Ring

Baked Rhubarb
and/or
Apple Fritters

Baked Fruit Cocktail

Coffee or Tea

Coconut Meringue Cake (see page 96)

Clear Tomato Soup

1 can tomatoes
2 cups cold water or stock
14 whole peppercorns
½ bay leaf
6 cloves
2 teaspoons sugar
1 slice onion
1½ teaspoons salt
⅛ teaspoon baking soda
2 tablespoons margarine
2 tablespoons flour

1 Combine tomatoes, stock, peppercorns, bay leaf, cloves, sugar and onion. Cook for 20 minutes.
2 Add salt and soda.
3 Thicken with margarine and flour.
4 Cook slowly for about 30 minutes, strain and serve.

Chicken with Fried Rice

2 cups chopped, cooked chicken
¼ cup oil
2 eggs, lightly beaten
1 teaspoon salt
⅛ teaspoon freshly ground black pepper
4 cups boiled rice
2 tablespoons soy sauce
3 scallions, chopped

1 Fry chicken in oil in a deep frying pan for 1 minute, stirring constantly. Do not overcook.
2 Add eggs, salt and pepper.
3 Fry this mixture over a medium heat for 5 minutes, stirring constantly.
4 Add rice and soy sauce and fry for 5 minutes; stirring frequently.
5 Add chopped scallions as a garnish.

Stuffed Mushroom Caps

½ lb medium to large mushrooms
½ cup (1 stick) corn oil margarine
2 small cloves garlic, minced
1 tablespoon parsley
¼ teaspoon salt
⅛ teaspoon freshly ground pepper

1 Wipe mushrooms with a damp cloth and break off stems.
2 Chop stems finely.
3 Combine softened margarine with minced garlic.
4 Add parsley and chopped stems and mix well.
5 Add salt and pepper to taste.
6 Fill mushroom caps generously with mixture.
7 Preheat oven to 450°F.
8 Bake in greased pan for 15 minutes.

Bing Cherry Ring

1 can pitted bing cherries
nuts
2 cups orange juice
1 cup sugar
3 tablespoons gelatin
1½ cups sherry
1 tablespoon oil to grease mold

1 Drain cherries and reserve juice. Stuff each cherry with a nut.
2 Mix cherry juice with 1½ cups orange juice and sugar, bring to the boil.
3 Soak gelatin in remaining orange juice and dissolve in hot juice. Add sherry.
4 Pour into greased mold.
5 When mixture begins to set in mold, add stuffed cherries and arrange in a pleasing design.

Linzer Torte (see page 105)

Baked Rhubarb

3 cups rhubarb
1 cup sugar
lemon rind

1 Carefully wash and dry rhubarb.
2 Cut rhubarb into 2 inch lengths and place in a baking dish.
3 Add sugar and a little lemon rind.
4 Cover and bake in a pre-heated oven at 350°F for 30-40 minutes or until tender.
5 Remove the lid for the last 10 minutes.

Apple Fritters

3 tart apples
¼ cup confectioners' sugar
2 tablespoons lemon juice

Fritter batter
1 cup flour
¼ teaspoon salt
1 egg, lightly beaten
½ cup water
1 tablespoon melted margarine

1 Peel and core apples and slice ¼ inch thick.
2 Sprinkle with sugar and diluted lemon juice.
3 Mix flour and salt.
4 Mix egg, water and margarine.
5 Add liquid mixture to flour and blend until smooth.
6 Dip slices of apple in the batter and fry in deep fat at 390°F.
7 Drain, sprinkle lightly with confectioners' sugar, and serve.

Baked Fruit Cocktail

3½ cups fruit cocktail
1 cup flour
1 cup sugar
1 teaspoon soda
¼ teaspoon salt
1 egg
brown sugar
chopped walnuts

1 Drain fruit cocktail for 1 hour.
2 Sift together dry ingredients several times, then add egg and beat well.
3 Combine with drained fruit cocktail until well mixed.
4 Spread in a greased pan.
5 Sprinkle brown sugar and nuts on top and bake in a pre-heated oven at 300°F for 45 minutes.
6 Cool and serve with peeled orange sections.

LUNCHEON

Menu No.23

Serves 6

Chilled Cherry Soup

Pineapple Surprise
and/or
Cod Casserole

Tangy Salad

Cauliflower Casserole
and/or
String Bean Fantastique

French Chocolate Dessert

Coffee or Tea

Chilled Cherry Soup

2 cups orange juice
1 can sour pitted cherries
1 tablespoon cornstarch
2 teaspoons of water
3 tablespoons sugar, or more if preferred
1 cinnamon stick

1 Drain cherries and retain juice. Combine cherry juice and orange juice and heat.
2 Make a paste of cornstarch and water.
3 Add to the fruit juices and bring to the boil.
4 Add sugar, cinnamon and cherries.
5 Boil for about 10 minutes.
6 Remove cinnamon stick.
7 Serve chilled.

Pineapple Surprise

½ lb pastrami, thinly sliced
2 cans pineapple chunks, drained

1 Preheat oven to 350°F.
2 Wrap 1 slice pastrami around each pineapple chunk and secure with a toothpick.
3 Bake for 10 minutes.

Cod Casserole

2 pounds cod
1 cup boiling, salted water
1 onion
1 green pepper
2 oz butter
½ cup breadcrumbs
1 teaspoon salt
⅛ teaspoon pepper
2 tablespoons chili sauce
1 can button mushrooms
1 small can tiny peas
milk

1 Cook cod in boiling, salted water with onion.
2 Sauté green pepper in melted butter.
3 Add breadcrumbs, salt, pepper and chili sauce to taste.
4 Bone fish, flake and add to mixture.
5 Add mushrooms and peas, including liquid from both cans.
6 Add as much milk as can be absorbed by this mixture.
7 Put in a greased casserole.
8 Sprinkle with breadcrumbs and dot with butter.
9 Bake in a pre-heated oven at 350°F until hot and browned.

Tangy Salad

2 packets lime gelatin
3¾ cups hot water
2 tablespoons vinegar
2 tablespoons grated onion
1 teaspoon salt
⅛ teaspoon pepper
½ cup sliced, scored cucumbers
1 cup cottage cheese
¼ cup finely diced green pepper
¼ cup finely diced carrot
¼ cup finely diced cucumber

1 Dissolve gelatin in hot water.
2 Add vinegar, grated onion, salt and pepper.
3 Turn 1 cup of mixture into 10 inch x 5 inch x 3 inch loaf pan and chill until slightly thickened.
4 Arrange the scored cucumbers in the mixture and chill until firm.
5 Chill remaining gelatin mixture until slightly thickened. To 1½ cups of mixture add cottage cheese and diced vegetables, and turn onto firm gelatin in the mold.
6 Pour remaining 1¼ cups of gelatin over cheese and vegetables layer.
7 Chill until firm.
8 Slice and serve on lettuce with mayonnaise.

Cauliflower Casserole

1 head of cauliflower, broken into
  flowerets
6 tablespoons seasoned breadcrumbs
¼ lb butter or margarine
8 eggs
⅛ teaspoon salt
⅛ teaspoon pepper
4 tablespoons sour cream
3 tablespoons Parmesan cheese

1 Cook cauliflower in salted water until
   tender.
2 Drain.
3 Brown breadcrumbs in butter or
   margarine in the casserole.
4 Toss cauliflower in the crumbs until each
   floweret is covered with the mixture.
5 Heat oven to 325°F.
6 Beat eggs lightly with salt, pepper and
   sour cream and pour over buttered cauliflower.
7 Bake for 30 minutes.
8 Sprinkle with Parmesan cheese and bake
   for 15-30 minutes longer until a wet knife
   inserted comes out dry, or almost dry
   (depending on the way you like your
   eggs).

String Bean Fantastique

2 packets frozen string beans (French
  cut), OR 1 lb fresh beans
½ cup cooking liquid
1 can cream of mushroom soup
1 can French fried onion rings

1 Cook string beans according to directions
   on packet. (Do not overcook.)
2 Drain, saving ½ cup liquid.
3 Put cooked string beans into a buttered
   casserole.
4 Add soup and liquid; stir.
5 Cover with onion rings.
6 Bake in a pre-heated oven at 375°F for
   about 25 minutes.

French Chocolate Dessert

4 ounces bitter chocolate
4 ounces sweet chocolate
2 cups sugar
8 eggs, separated
1 quart heavy cream

Garnish
6 maraschino cherries

1 Melt chocolate in the top of a double
   boiler.
2 Blend sugar with beaten egg yolks. Add
   to the chocolate mixture.
3 Fold in beaten whites.
4 Whip the cream and add to the chocolate
   mixture.
5 Refrigerate before serving.
6 Garnish with a maraschino cherry.

LUNCHEON

No. 24

Serves 4

Carrot and Pea Soup

Marinated Mushrooms
and/or
Baked Beef Stew

Avocado Salad

Armenian Rice Pilaf
and/or
Broiled Tomatoes

Brandied Hot Cherries

Almond Horns

Coffee or Tea

Carrot and Pea Soup

2 tablespoons corn oil margarine
1 teaspoon salt
⅛ teaspoon pepper
⅛ teaspoon thyme
1 medium onion, finely diced
1 clove garlic, minced
2 cans pea soup
2 cans chicken or beef bouillon
2 medium, raw carrots

1 Place margarine, salt, pepper and thyme in a heavy iron saucepan.
2 Add onion and garlic.
3 Cover and cook gently for a few minutes until onion is soft but not brown.
4 Add pea soup.
5 Rinse out the soup cans with the bouillon, and blend it in gradually.
6 Bring to boiling point, stirring constantly.
7 Finely shave the carrots on the slicer end of your vegetable grater.
8 Add to the soup and serve.

Marinated Mushrooms

10-15 small mushroom caps, fresh or canned
lettuce leaves

Marinade
¼ cup salad oil
¼-½ cup cider vinegar
1 tablespoon finely chopped onion
1 tablespoon finely chopped parsley
1 clove garlic, crushed
¼ teaspoon salt
¼ teaspoon sugar

1 Wash mushrooms.
2 Combine marinade ingredients and add mushrooms.
3 Cover and refrigerate for at least 2 hours.
4 Drain mushrooms and serve on lettuce leaves.

Baked Beef Stew

2 lb stew beef, cubed
1 can tiny peas
1 cup sliced carrots
2 chopped onions
1 teaspoon salt
⅛ teaspoon pepper
1 bay leaf
1 large raw potato, sliced thinly
1 x 15 oz can tomato sauce
½ cup white wine

1 Combine ingredients and mix well in a casserole.
2 Cover tightly with the lid.
3 Bake in pre-heated oven at 275°F for 5 hours.
4 Serve on a bed of pilaf rice.

Avocado Salad

1 alligator pear (avocado)
2 slices pineapple, fresh or canned
4 lettuce leaves
1 teaspoon salt
¼ teaspoon paprika
2 tablespoons lemon juice
1 teaspoon lime juice

1 Peel alligator pear and cut pulp into small pieces.
2 Cut pineapple into cubes.
3 Arrange on crisp lettuce leaves.
4 Mix remaining ingredients and pour over the fruit.

Armenian Rice Pilaf

1 tablespoon vegetable oil
¼ cup very fine egg noodles
1 cup uncooked long-grain rice
salt
⅛ teaspoon freshly ground pepper
¼ cup margarine
2 cups boiling chicken stock, canned or fresh

115

1 Preheat oven to 325°F.
2 Heat oil in a flameproof casserole and cook noodles until lightly browned.
3 Add rice, salt, pepper, margarine and chicken stock.
4 Stir over a low heat until margarine melts.
5 Cover tightly and bake for 25-30 minutes or until all the liquid is absorbed.
6 Remove casserole from the oven and take off the lid.
7 Cover the casserole with a kitchen towel, replace the lid and stand aside for 5 minutes.
Note: Armenian Rice Pilaf can be made earlier in the day and reheated.

Broiled Tomatoes

1 tablespoon softened margarine
1 hard-cooked egg yolk, mashed
1 teaspoon lime juice
1 teaspoon prepared mustard
⅛ teaspoon salt
4 tomatoes

1 Blend margarine, egg yolk, lime juice, mustard and salt.
2 Cut off the top third of each tomato.
3 Spread mixture over cut tomato.
4 Put tomatoes under the broiler and broil for 4-5 minutes.
5 Serve hot.

Brandied Hot Cherries

1 large can pitted black cherries
juice of 1 large orange
grated rind of 1 orange
2-3 tablespoons brown sugar
2 tablespoons margarine
4 oz Cointreau or apricot brandy

1 Drain cherries and place in a baking dish or chafing dish.
2 Add orange juice, rind, brown sugar and margarine.

3 Heat through but do not boil.
4 Pour over Cointreau or apricot brandy and serve.
Note: Fresh cherries can be substituted.

Almond Horns

½ lb margarine
2 oz vanilla powdered sugar
¼ lb grated almonds
1 cup flour
vanilla powdered sugar (extra)

1 Cream margarine, add sugar and blend well.
2 Gradually add grated almonds, then work in flour.
3 Place dough in the refrigerator until ready to use. (If in a hurry chilling is not absolutely necessary, but it improves the texture.)
4 Take pieces of dough the size of a walnut and roll into balls. Press balls into finger shapes and bend into crescents.
5 Place on a cookie sheet and bake in a pre-heated oven at 425°F until a golden brown.
6 Place some vanilla sugar in a small bowl and dip the top of each crescent while hot into the sugar.
Note: Vanilla sugar is made by cutting up a vanilla bean and keeping it in a jar of powdered sugar. When all the sugar is used, the remaining bean can be used again.

LUNCHEON

No. 25

Serves 4

Split Pea Soup

Appetizer Puffs
and/or
Beef and Fish Fondue

Majestic Salad Ring

Brussel Sprouts Lyonnaise
and/or
Eggplant Timbales

Apricot Whip

Delicious Cookies

Coffee or Tea

Split Pea Soup

1½ lb flanken and bones
3 quarts water
1 large onion, minced
1½ cups split peas, green or yellow
1 teaspoon salt
dash pepper
1 carrot
2 stalks celery
½ cup tomato juice

1 Trim meat and bones of all fat.
2 Put into water with minced onion and bring to the boil.
3 Skim off the fat, lower the heat, and add split peas and seasonings.
4 Simmer for 1 hour.
5 Add carrot, celery and tomato juice and simmer for 30 minutes or until peas have dissolved.

Appetizer Puffs

½ cup shortening
1 cup water
1½ cups flour
5 eggs

1 Put shortening and water in a saucepan and bring to the boil.
2 Add flour and mix well.
3 Cook for 2 minutes, stirring constantly.
4 Cool. Add eggs one at a time, beating after each egg is added.
5 Beat for 5 minutes.
6 Drop spoonfuls of mixture about 2 inches apart on a shallow, greased pan.
7 Shape into rounds, leaving the centers a little higher than the rest.
8 Bake in a pre-heated oven at 350°F for 30 minutes.
9 Cool. Make a slit with sharp pointed knife near the bottom of puff and fill with chopped liver paste, or caviar and egg mixture.

Beef and Fish Fondue

peanut oil
2 lb beef, cut into 1 inch cubes
8 tiny meatballs
4 frankfurters, cut into chunks
2 lb halibut, cut into chunks

Sweet 'n Tangy Sauce
1 tablespoon cornstarch
½ cup orange juice
½ cup honey
¼ cup yellow mustard
¼ teaspoon ground ginger

Chateaubriand Sauce
1 envelope brown gravy mix
½ cup water
¼ cup dry white wine
2 tablespoons margarine

Curried Mayonnaise Sauce
1½ cups mayonnaise
¼ teaspoon dry mustard
1 tablespoon curry powder

1 Half fill fondue pot with peanut oil. Place over a high heat.
2 When oil is hot set fondue pot over the burner on the serving table.
3 Each person spears pieces of meat or fish on a fondue fork, holds it in the oil until cooked, then dips it in one of the sauces.
4 To make Sweet 'n Tangy Sauce, combine cornstarch and orange juice in a small saucepan, stirring constantly until blended.
5 Add honey, mustard and ginger.
6 Heat to boiling point until thick.
7 Serve Sweet 'n Tangy Sauce in a small bowl.
8 To make Chateaubriand Sauce combine gravy mix, water, wine and margarine in a small saucepan.
9 Heat to boiling point, stirring frequently.
10 Serve Chateaubriand Sauce in a small bowl.
11 To make Curried Mayonnaise Sauce mix mayonnaise, dry mustard and curry powder, stirring well.

12 Serve Curried Mayonnaise Sauce in a
small bowl.
Note: Provide 1 fondue pot for every 4
people.

Majestic Salad Ring

3 packets lemon gelatin
3 cups hot water
1 can crushed pineapple
2 cups pineapple juice from can
1 cup chopped nutmeats
1 cup chopped celery
1 small jar sweet pickle relish
1 small jar pimiento-stuffed olives
1 cup seedless grapes, halved and peeled

1 Dissolve gelatin in water.
2 Drain pineapple and retain 2 cups of juice.
(If there isn't quite enough, make up the
difference with water.)
3 Add other ingredients. Mix well and turn
into a mold.
4 Serve with Thousand Island Dressing.
Note: You can also combine tuna, diced
apples, lemon juice, chopped celery and salad
dressing and place this mixture in the center of
the mold when it is turned out.

Brussel Sprouts Lyonnaise

1 medium onion
3 tablespoons fat or margarine
¼ cup bouillon
1 lb Brussel sprouts
salt
paprika
3 tablespoons chopped parsley

1 Dice and sauté onion in fat or margarine.
2 Add bouillon and Brussel sprouts.
3 Season to taste with salt and paprika.
4 Simmer ingredients, stirring frequently
until bouillon has evaporated.
5 Sprinkle with chopped parsley.
6 Serve very hot.

Eggplant Timbales

1 eggplant, pared and cut into ¼ inch
slices
¼ cup margarine
½ cup soft breadcrumbs
2 eggs, well beaten
few drops onion juice
½ teaspoon salt
⅛ teaspoon pepper
canned pimientos
margarined crumbs
parsley

1 Cook eggplant in boiling, salted water
until soft.
2 Drain thoroughly, cut and mash.
3 Add margarine, breadcrumbs, eggs, onion
juice, salt and pepper.
4 Line small greased molds or custard cups
with pimientos.
5 Fill molds with mixture and sprinkle top
with margarined crumbs.
6 Bake in a pre-heated oven for 15 minutes
at 375°F.
7 Remove from molds and garnish with
parsley.
Note: Eggplant mixture may also be baked in
a baking dish.

Apricot Whip

2 egg whites
¾ cup cooked, puréed apricots
2 tablespoons juice from apricots
¼ cup sugar
⅛ teaspoon salt
1 teaspoon brandy extract (optional)

1 Make sure egg whites are at room
temperature.
2 Put all ingredients in a mixing bowl.
3 Beat at medium speed until mixture
becomes thick and fluffy and stands in
peaks.
4 Scrape fruit from beaters and sides of the
bowl.

5 Beat for 5 minutes more.
6 Serve immediately with Delicious Cookies. (This dessert will hold for about 1 hour when refrigerated.)

Delicious Cookies

1¾ cups cake flour
1 teaspoon baking powder
⅛ teaspoon salt
2 tablespoons sugar
½ cup margarine
2 eggs, separated
juice and grated rind of ½ lemon

1 cup sugar
½ cup walnuts
powdered sugar

1 Sift flour, baking powder, salt and 2 tablespoons sugar.
2 Cut margarine into mixture.
3 Add egg yolks, lemon juice and rind and blend.
4 Refrigerate for 1 hour or more.
5 Roll dough out on a floured board.
6 Cut into squares or oblongs, cover with lightly beaten egg whites, sugar and walnuts.
7 Bake in a pre-heated oven at 350°F.
8 Dust with powdered sugar and serve.

LUNCHEON

Menu

No.26

Serves 8

Mushroom-Barley Soup
and/or
Fruit Cocktail

Essig Fleisch

Beet Ring

Stuffed Turnips
and/or
Potato Pirogen

Sponge Cake

Coffee or Tea

Mushroom-Barley Soup

2 oz dried mushrooms
¼ cup lima beans
2 tablespoons barley
2 carrots, diced
1 onion
2 stalks celery
2 cans tomatoes
3 quarts water
1 lb beef and bones

1 Soak mushrooms and beans.
2 Wash barley.
3 Clean vegetables.
4 Combine all ingredients and cover.
5 Bring to the boil and simmer for 3 hours.

Fruit Cocktail

2 bananas
1 cup canned pineapple
2 oranges
1 dozen maraschino cherries
8 tablespoons maraschino cherry juice
8 teaspoons lemon juice
1 teaspoon powdered sugar

1 Peel and dice bananas.
2 Dice pineapple.
3 Remove the pulp from oranges, and cut each section into several pieces.
4 Cut cherries in half and combine with the fruit.
5 Place mixture on ice until thoroughly chilled.
6 Spoon mixture into cocktail glasses. Add 1 tablespoon maraschino juice and 1 teaspoonful lemon juice to each glass.
7 Sprinkle with powdered sugar and serve.

Essig Fleisch

3 lb boneless chuck beef, cut into small pieces
2-3 onions, finely chopped

1 x 15 oz can tomato sauce
2 cups water
¼ teaspoon sugar
⅛ teaspoon salt

1 Sauté meat and onions.
2 Cover and cook without water until browned. (Meat will draw its own juice.)
3 Uncover and let liquid reduce until meat browns.
4 Add tomato sauce.
5 Pour water over meat.
6 Add sugar and salt and cook 2-3 hours or until meat is tender.

Beet Ring

2 packets raspberry gelatin
beet juice from can
1 large can whole beets, grated
½ bottle horseradish
lemon juice

1 Make gelatin according to directions on packet, using half beet juice and water.
2 Add beets and horseradish and mix together.
3 Taste and add lemon juice.
4 Put in a ring mold and refrigerate.

Stuffed Turnips

8 medium turnips
salt and pepper
½ cup almonds, shredded
1 teaspoon salt
2 eggs
⅛ teaspoon nutmeg
⅛ teaspoon freshly ground pepper
¼ cup breadcrumbs
2 tablespoons melted margarine

1 Wash and cook turnips in water with salt and pepper until tender.
2 When cool, peel and scoop out centers.

3 Mash and add almonds, salt, eggs, nutmeg and pepper.
4 Stuff the turnips.
5 Sprinkle with margarined breadcrumbs.
6 Place in an oiled pan and bake till light brown, basting often with melted margarine.

Potato Pirogen

1½ cups flour
½ teaspoon salt
½ cup shortening
¼ cup cold water
3 tablespoons melted margarine

Potato filling
1 medium onion, diced
1 tablespoon chicken fat
2 cups mashed cooked potato
½ teaspoon salt
½ teaspoon pepper
1 egg, lightly beaten

1 Sift flour and salt together.
2 Cut shortening into flour.
3 Work water into dough 1 tablespoon at a time.
4 Roll dough out to ⅛ inch thick and cut into 4 inch squares.
5 Brown onion in fat.
6 Combine with other filling ingredients and mix thoroughly.
7 Put a little filling into each square of dough.
8 Fold into a pocket shape and pinch edges together.
9 Place on a greased pan.
10 Brush tops with melted margarine.
11 Bake in a pre-heated oven at 425°F for 20 minutes.

Sponge Cake

1 cup cake flour, sifted
1 cup sugar, sifted
5 egg yolks
1½ teaspoons grated lemon rind
1½ tablespoons lemon juice
¼ teaspoon salt
5 egg whites

1 Sift flour, measure, add ¼ cup of the sugar and sift again.
2 Beat egg yolks until thick and lemon colored.
3 Add lemon rind and juice and beat until thick and light.
4 Add salt to egg whites and beat until stiff enough to hold peaks, but not dry.
5 Add remaining sugar, 2 tablespoons at a time, beating after each addition until sugar is just blended.
6 Fold in egg yolks.
7 Sift flour over eggs, about ¼ cup at a time, and fold in lightly.
8 Pour into an ungreased 9 inch tube pan and bake in a pre-heated oven at 325°F for 60-70 minutes.
9 Turn cake pan upside down on a cake rack until thoroughly cool.

DINNER
MENUS

All human history attests
That happiness for man—the hungry sinner—
Since Eve ate apples, much depends on dinner!
Byron *Don Juan* Canto XIII

AN adage in our home was: No matter how difficult the day, or how high or low the spirit, the bridge to pleasure was the warmth of food and the joy of sharing it with others. These twenty-six dinners, presented as totally planned meals, are designed to accommplish this also. Meals should be social happenings. I am aware that you will not always have occasion to break bread with your friends and associates, so on those occasions when you do, it should be memorable.

Each meal is intended to be pleasing to the eye and rewarding to the palate. Color in food presentation is of paramount importance, and plate arrangement plays a dramatic part in visual appreciation. A delicious aroma will tantalize your sense of smell and a meal can produce a bewitching effect. Variety of texture is also important.

There is no rule that says you must follow each menu as if it were a commandment. To make the kind of meal you want, exchange dishes from other menus; but be careful to maintain the balance of the meal. Note the blending of color, tone, texture and aroma. And when you make changes try to visualize these factors and take fullest advantage of all the elements. As in the luncheon menus, you again have a series of and/or choices.

Cooking gives you the chance to become an artist producing a memorable creation. Cooking a delicious meal is an accomplishment that should make you proud. Enjoy every minute of it, and share your enjoyment with others.

Veal in Black Olives (see page 175)

DINNER

Menu No.1

Serves 8

Mushroom and Barley Soup

Bermuda Onion Pie
and/or
Lamb Shashlik

Sliced Pickled Beet Molded Salad
and/or
Brown Rice

Cooked Cucumber

Open Peach Cake

Coffee or Tea

Open Peach Cake (see page 129)

Mushroom and Barley Soup

¾ cup pearl barley
2 quarts soup stock
½ lb mushrooms, chopped
½ grated onion
2 tablespoons margarine
1 tablespoon minced parsley
salt and pepper

1 Simmer barley in half the soup stock until soft.
2 Sauté chopped mushrooms and onions in margarine until onions are transparent.
3 Add to the barley with the remaining stock, parsley, salt and pepper.
4 Boil for 10 minutes.
5 Serve with toasted croutons.

Bermuda Onion Pie

3 large Bermuda onions
margarine
1 egg
½ pint sour cream substitute
⅛ teaspoon salt
⅛ teaspoon pepper
1 x 8-9 inch baked pie crust, cooled

1 Cut the onions in half and then slice into semi-circles.
2 Sauté in margarine in a covered pan until soft but not brown.
3 Cool.
4 Beat egg well and add sour cream substitute, pepper and salt.
5 Add the cooled onions to sour cream mixture, and pour into baked pie crust.
6 Bake in a pre-heated oven at 350°F for about 30 minutes or until the top is brown and dry.

Note: The filling should not be too dry when cooked. (It should be like a Yorkshire pudding.)

Lamb Shashlik

1 cup red wine
¼ cup olive oil
2 cloves garlic, crushed
1 tablespoon salt
freshly ground pepper
1 teaspoon oregano
4-5 lb lamb, cut in 2 inch cubes
16 small white onions
1 green pepper, cubed
16 cherry tomatoes
1 eggplant, cut into cubes
16 mushroom caps

1 Combine the wine, olive oil, garlic cloves, salt, ground pepper and oregano.
2 Marinate meat overnight in this mixture.
3 String meat on skewers.
4 Place vegetables on separate skewers.
5 Brush with marinade and cook on a hot grill or under a broiler.
6 Cook meat first, as the vegetables take less time to cook.

Sliced Pickled Beet Molded Salad

1 envelope gelatin
¼ cup cold water
1 cup boiling water
¾ cup cold water
¼ cup lemon juice
½ teaspoon salt
½ teaspoon onion juice
pickled beets

1 Dissolve gelatin in cold water for five minutes.
2 Then stir into boiling water until thoroughly dissolved.
3 Add cold water, lemon juice, salt and onion juice.
4 Arrange mold or molds rinsed in cold water in a pan of ice or ice water.
5 Pour a layer of gelatin into the mold.

When set, lay on thin slices of well drained pickled beets, then another layer of gelatin.

6 Repeat till mold is full. Finish with a layer of gelatin on top.
7 Chill until firm.
8 When ready to serve, turn out on bed of French endive or watercress.

Brown Rice

2 onions, finely diced
3 tablespoons oil
2 cups white rice
2 cups boiling water
2 beef bouillon cubes
salt and pepper to taste

1 Sauté onions in oil.
2 When soft, add rice mixed with water and bouillon cubes.
3 Bring to the boil, then turn heat to low and put lid across $\frac{1}{2}$ of saucepan.
4 Cook for about 18-20 minutes or until water is absorbed.
5 Season to taste with salt and pepper.

Cooked Cucumber

4 cucumbers
$\frac{1}{2}$ cup water
$\frac{1}{8}$ teaspoon salt
$\frac{1}{8}$ teaspoon pepper
2 tablespoons margarine

1 Peel cucumbers.
2 Cut in rounds half an inch thick.
3 Put in saucepan with water and simmer until cucumbers are tender (test with a fork).
4 Season with salt and pepper.
5 Just before serving add margarine.

Open Peach Cake

$1\frac{1}{2}$ cups sifted flour
1 teaspoon baking powder
$\frac{1}{2}$ teaspoon salt
2 tablespoons sugar
$\frac{1}{2}$ cup margarine
1 egg yolk
2 tablespoons water
4 cups sliced apples or peaches

Topping
$\frac{1}{2}$ cup sugar

2 tablespoons margarine
$1\frac{1}{2}$ tablespoons flour
$\frac{1}{8}$ teaspoon salt

1 Sift dry ingredients.
2 Work in shortening until well blended.
3 Mix egg yolk with water and add to mixture.
4 Grease 8 inch square cake pan and line with this dough.
5 Cover with sliced apples or peaches.
6 Combine topping ingredients and spread over apples or peaches.
7 Bake in a pre-heated oven at 400°F for 45-60 minutes.
8 Serve hot.

DINNER

No.2

Serves 4

Asparagus Soup

Sweet and Sour Meatballs
and/or
Steak Orientale

Nut and Olive Salad

Peas with Water Chestnuts
and/or
Brown Rice Bed

Pears in Curaçao

Dutch Butter Cookies

Coffee or Tea

Asparagus Soup

2 lb asparagus
2 cans mushroom soup, strained
⅛ teaspoon salt
⅛ teaspoon pepper

1 Boil asparagus for about 20 minutes. Save the concentrated liquid.
2 Put asparagus through a sieve, or pureé in a blender. Add the cooking liquid.
3 Mix strained soup with the asparagus mixture.
4 Season and serve.

Sweet and Sour Meatballs

1 lb ground beef
½ cup water
½ cup matzo meal
1 egg, lightly beaten
¼ cup minced onion
½ teaspoon salt
¼ teaspoon pepper
1 large onion, diced
¼ cup lemon juice
½ cup sugar
8 oz can tomato and mushroom sauce
½ cup water

1 Mix meat, water, matzo meal, eggs, minced onion, salt and pepper.
2 Shape into meatballs.
3 Mix diced onion, lemon juice, sugar, tomato and mushroom sauce and water.
4 Cook large meatballs in this sauce for 1 hour or small meatballs for 40 minutes.
5 Serve with sauce spooned over meatballs.

Steak Orientale

1½ lb tender steak, cut very thinly
  beef suet
4 stalks celery, cut diagonally into ½ inch pieces
½ bunch scallions, cut in 1 inch pieces

1 packet frozen chopped spinach
1 can bean sprouts
½ lb fresh mushrooms, sliced
1 bunch watercress sprigs

Sauce
¼ cup soy sauce
2 tablespoons white wine or sherry
½ cup water
4 teaspoons sugar
1 clove garlic, crushed
1 cube beef broth concentrate

1 Place an electric skillet on the dinner table and set at 260°F.
2 Put half the meat in the skillet with a piece of beef suet.
3 Combine sauce ingredients in a separate jug.
4 Add half the sauce to meat.
5 Add half the vegetables, adding mushrooms and watercress last.
6 Cook for 5-6 minutes, or until spinach has separated.
7 Serve over rice.
8 Cook the remaining ingredients.

Nut and Olive Salad

1 packet lemon gelatin
1 small bottle stuffed olives
1 cup chopped nuts
1 hard-cooked egg, finely chopped

1 Combine all ingredients and pour into a lightly greased mold and chill.
2 Cut into wedges and serve.

Peas with Water Chestnuts

1 x 10 oz packet frozen peas
¼ teaspoon sugar
¼ cup boiling water
1 cup water chestnuts, thinly sliced
½ tablespoon chopped fresh mint, OR ½ teaspoon dried mint

⅛ cup Grand Marnier
¼ cup margarine
1 teaspoon salt

1 Add peas and sugar to boiling water in
  large saucepan.
2 Bring to the boil, and gently separate peas
  with a fork.
3 Reduce heat: simmer uncovered for 5
  minutes.
4 Drain peas.
5 Add remaining ingredients.
6 Toss lightly to mix well.
7 Reheat gently and serve.

Brown Rice Bed

2 cups boiling water
2 tablespoons margarine
½ teaspoon salt
⅛ teaspoon pepper
1 cup brown rice
4 mushrooms, finely chopped
1 tablespoon chopped parsley

1 In a saucepan bring water, margarine, salt
  and pepper to the boil.
2 When water is boiling add rice.
3 Stir twice, reduce heat to low and cook
  for 45 minutes, half covered.
4 After 35 minutes add mushrooms and
  parsley.
5 Cook for 10 minutes or until rice is soft
  and water absorbed.
6 Serve with steak.

Pears in Curaçao

1 large can Bartlett pear halves
¼ cup powdered sugar
1 teaspoon lemon juice
1 teaspoon orange juice
2 teaspoons Curaçao
1 teaspoon kirsch
⅛ teaspoon salt

1 Chill pears.
2 Combine remaining ingredients and stir
  until no longer granular.
3 Pour over pear halves.

Dutch Butter Cookies

½ lb margarine
2 cups flour
1 cup sugar
1 egg

1 Knead all ingredients together till smooth.
2 Pat in a thin layer on a cookie sheet.
3 Bake in a moderate oven for about 10
  minutes or until brown.
4 Remove from oven. Cut into diamond
  shapes while hot.
5 Remove carefully from pan.

DINNER

Menu

No.3

Serves 8

Onion Soup

Mushroom Canapé
and/or
Fillet of Sole in Cream Sauce

Roquefort and Tomato Aspic Ring

Baked Asparagus
and/or
Squash au Gratin

Plum Kuchen

Coffee or Tea

Onion Soup

4 large onions, sliced
4 tablespoons butter
1 can beef bouillon
1 can consommé
$\frac{1}{8}$ teaspoon salt
$\frac{1}{8}$ teaspoon pepper
2 cans water
$\frac{1}{4}$ cup grated Parmesan cheese
extra Parmesan cheese for serving

1 Sauté onions in butter until they are light brown.
2 Combine all ingredients, including Parmesan cheese, in a greased casserole.
3 Cover.
4 Bake for 1 hour in a pre-heated oven at 350°F.
5 Serve with a dish of Parmesan cheese.

Mushroom Canapé

$\frac{1}{2}$ lb mushrooms, sliced
1 large onion, finely diced
$\frac{1}{4}$ cup flour
salt and pepper to taste
$\frac{1}{4}$ cup sweet cream or milk
$\frac{1}{2}$ large loaf white sandwich bread
2 oz melted butter
grated Parmesan cheese

1 Sauté mushrooms and onion in butter.
2 Add flour, salt, pepper and cream to make a lumpy paste.
3 Trim crusts from bread and slice.
4 Roll slices of bread flat with a rolling pin.
5 Spread mixture thinly on bread.
6 Roll up bread slices.
7 Refrigerate for 24 hours.
8 Cut each roll in 4 parts.
9 Dip in melted butter.
10 Roll in Parmesan cheese.
11 Bake in a pre-heated oven at 350°F until brown.
12 Serve hot.

Fillet of Sole in Cream Sauce

1 lb spinach
$\frac{1}{8}$ teaspoon salt
$\frac{1}{8}$ teaspoon pepper
2 lb fillets of sole
1 slice of lemon
1 onion, sliced
sprig of parsley

Cream sauce
2 tablespoons butter
2 tablespoons flour
1 cup milk
Parmesan cheese
salt and pepper

1 Thoroughly wash spinach.
2 Put in a saucepan with no more water than clings to the leaves.
3 Cook for 10 minutes.
4 Drain, finely chop and season with salt and pepper.
5 Cover fillets of sole with water adding lemon, onion and parsley.
6 Simmer for 10 minutes and drain.
7 Put spinach in the bottom of a buttered casserole and top with fillets.
8 Melt 2 tablespoons of butter in a saucepan.
9 Add flour and blend.
10 Stir with wooden spoon until lightly browned.
11 Add 1 cup milk slowly, stirring constantly.
12 When mixture starts to thicken, remove from heat.
13 Add Parmesan cheese, and salt and pepper to taste.
14 Bake in a pre-heated oven at 350°F for 30 minutes or until sauce has browned.

Roquefort and Tomato Aspic Ring

2 tablespoons gelatin
4 tablespoons cold water
1 cup boiling water
1 teaspoon salt
3 cups tomatoes or tomato juice
2 thick slices onion
2 bay leaves
4 celery leaves
4 whole cloves
1 teaspoon sugar
2 tablespoons vinegar

Cheese mixture
½ lb Roquefort cheese
thick cream
½ cup chopped nuts
½ cup chopped ripe olives

1 Soak gelatin in cold water.
2 Mix all the other ingredients, except the vinegar and cheese mixture ingredients. Cook slowly in a covered pan for 20 minutes.
3 Press through a strainer or purée in a blender.
4 Heat to boiling point and add gelatin mixture.
5 Stir until gelatin is thoroughly dissolved.
6 Cool, then add vinegar.
7 Pour into a ring mold.
8 While this is cooling, cream Roquefort cheese with thick cream until smooth. Add chopped nuts and chopped ripe olives.
9 When the aspic is cold, layer the Roquefort mixture over the aspic.
10 Chill and serve with a variety of vegetables and crisp salad greens.

Baked Asparagus

2 lb asparagus
2 tablespoons chopped green pepper
2 cups medium white sauce
6 hard-cooked eggs, sliced
½ cup buttered crumbs

1 Cook asparagus until tender.
2 Add pepper to white sauce.
3 Arrange layer of asparagus in the bottom of a greased casserole; cover generously with sauce.
4 Add layer of egg slices.
5 Repeat until dish is full.
6 Cover with buttered crumbs and bake in a pre-heated oven at 350°F for 20 minutes.

Squash au Gratin

1½ lb young yellow squash OR 5 small squash
4 tablespoons butter
⅛ teaspoon salt
⅛ teaspoon pepper
¼ teaspoon sugar
2 eggs, well beaten
½ lb American cheese, grated
½ cup breadcrumbs

1 Cut and boil squash until tender.
2 Drain in a colander and mash.
3 Add butter, season with salt and pepper and a dash of sugar.
4 Add eggs and grated cheese.
5 Pour into a large buttered Pyrex baking dish; cover with breadcrumbs.
6 Bake in a pre-heated oven at 325°F for about 20 minutes.

Plum Kuchen

¼ lb butter or margarine
1 teaspoon baking powder
1 egg yolk
1½ cups flour
¼ teaspoon salt
¼ cup milk
15 Italian blue plums
¼ cup brown sugar

1 Blend butter, baking powder, egg yolk, flour and salt.
2 Add milk to moisten batter so it will stick together.
3 When it forms a ball, press evenly into a greased square Pyrex baking dish.
4 Cut Italian blue plums in half and arrange on top of batter.
5 Press fruit in firmly, sprinkle with brown sugar.
6 Bake for 1 hour in a pre-heated oven at 350°F.

Note: Apricots or peach halves can be substituted if Italian blue plums are unavailable.

DINNER

Menu No.4

Serves 4

Pea Soup with Dumplings

Chicken Livers and Wild Rice
and/or
Duck Rotisserie

Waldorf Salad

Jambalaya
and/or
Barley Casserole

Stewed Rhubarb and Strawberries

Floating Meringue Kisses

Coffee or Tea

Pea Soup with Dumplings

2 lb green peas in their pods
3 tablespoons margarine
2 tablespoons flour
$\frac{1}{8}$ teaspoon salt
$\frac{1}{8}$ teaspoon pepper
1 teaspoon beef extract

Dumplings
4 tablespoons margarine
$\frac{1}{2}$ cup flour
1 cup water
2 eggs, separated
chopped parsley

1 Shell peas. Place pea pods in a saucepan, cover and boil. Strain off cooking water and retain. Discard the pods.
2 Put peas into a saucepan with 2 tablespoons margarine and cover with water. Cook until tender.
3 Combine the peas and the two lots of cooking water. Add more water if necessary to make 3 pints.
4 Add flour and 1 tablespoon of margarine, salt, pepper and beef extract. Bring to the boil.
5 Using dumpling ingredients, cook margarine, flour and water until thick and smooth; cool. Add egg yolks and stiffly beaten whites.
6 Blend well.
7 Drop spoonfuls of mixture into soup. When dumplings rise to the top add chopped parsley and serve.

Chicken Livers and Wild Rice

1 cup wild rice
2 cups chicken broth
$\frac{1}{2}$ cup margarine
3 small onions, finely chopped
1 clove garlic
$\frac{1}{4}$ lb mushrooms, sliced
$\frac{3}{4}$ lb chicken livers

3 tablespoons cognac or sherry
$\frac{1}{4}$ teaspoon nutmeg
$\frac{3}{4}$ teaspoon thyme
$\frac{1}{8}$ teaspoon salt
$\frac{1}{8}$ teaspoon pepper

1 Prepare rice according to directions using chicken broth for final cooking.
2 Heat margarine in skillet.
3 Sauté onions and garlic until tender, not browned.
4 Add mushrooms and cook for 3 minutes.
5 Increase heat.
6 Add livers and brown quickly on all sides.
7 Add cognac and stir to loosen cooked-on particles.
8 Add cooked rice and toss to mix.
9 Reheat mixture.
10 Season with nutmeg, thyme, salt and pepper.

Duck Rotisserie

5-6 lb duckling
$\frac{1}{8}$ teaspoon salt
8 sprigs parsley
$\frac{1}{2}$ lemon
$\frac{1}{4}$ cup dark molasses
$\frac{1}{2}$ cup soy sauce
$\frac{1}{2}$ cup sherry
1 clove garlic, minced

1 Wash and dry duck inside and out.
2 Sprinkle cavity with salt and insert parsley and lemon.
3 Truss bird securely.
4 In a saucepan combine molasses, soy sauce, sherry and garlic. Cook over a low heat for 5 minutes.
5 Insert spit rod through center of duckling.
6 Roast for about 2 hours or until tender, basting every 15 minutes with sauce.

Waldorf Salad

4 tasty apples
1 tablespoon sugar
juice of $\frac{1}{4}$ lemon

¼ cup walnuts
¼ cup raisins
½ cup mayonnaise

1 Pare and cube apples.
2 Add sugar, lemon juice, walnuts, raisins and mayonnaise.
3 Mix with 2 forks until blended.
4 Chill and serve.

Jambalaya

1 large onion, minced
¼ clove garlic, finely chopped
1 green pepper, chopped
2 tablespoons margarine
3½ cups tomatoes
3 cups boiling water
1 cup uncooked rice
1 teaspoon salt
dash pepper

1 Sauté onion, garlic and green pepper in margarine for 5 minutes.
2 Add tomatoes and water and heat till boiling.
3 Add rice and seasonings, cover and simmer for 20 minutes or until rice is tender and moisture almost absorbed.

Barley Casserole

½ cup raw barley (medium or very fine)
2 tablespoons margarine
2 cups onion soup (use dehydrated variety)
¼ pound mushrooms, sliced
2 tablespoons diced almonds
½ cup bouillon

1 Brown barley in a heavy skillet in one half of the margarine.
2 Remove barley and mix with 1 cup of soup; reserve one cup of soup.
3 Sauté mushrooms in remaining margarine. Mix in almonds and add to barley and soup mixture.

4 Pour into a 3 quart margarined casserole.
5 Cover and bake in a pre-heated oven at 375°F for 45 minutes, stirring occasionally.
6 Add reserved onion soup.
7 Remove cover and bake for about ½ hour more or until barley is soft.
8 Add bouillon and serve.

Stewed Rhubarb and Strawberries

4 stalks rhubarb
1 cup sugar
½ cup water
4 cups strawberries

1 Wash rhubarb thoroughly.
2 Cut into 1 inch slices.
3 Add ½ cup sugar and water.
4 Bring to the boil and cook quickly until tender.
5 Clean, hull and wash strawberries.
6 Drop strawberries into cooking rhubarb and add remaining sugar.
7 Stew for 5 minutes.
8 Cool and serve.

Floating Meringue Kisses

3 egg whites
1 cup granulated sugar, sifted
1 teaspoon vinegar
1 teaspoon vanilla extract

1 Beat egg whites slowly, then increase beating speed until they are stiff and dry.
2 Add sugar gradually as you continue to beat.
3 Add vinegar and vanilla and beat well.
4 Drop spoonfuls of mixture onto a baking sheet covered with smooth glazed paper.
5 Leave about 1 inch between kisses.
6 Bake in a pre-heated oven at 250°F for 20 minutes.

DINNER

No. 5

Serves 6

Onion Soup
and/or
Antipasto

**Sole and Salmon Rolls
with Piquant Sauce**

Orange-Cranberry Mold

Cauliflower Pimiento Sauce
and/or
Stuffed Zucchini

Divine Pie

Coffee or Tea

Onion Soup

8 onions
1 cup water
½ cup of margarine
1 tablespoon flour
2 quarts rich soup stock
1 tablespoon salt

1 Slice onions into rings and cook in water until the water is absorbed.
2 Add margarine and fry slowly until brown.
3 Add flour.
4 Add onion mixture to soup stock. Add salt and simmer slowly in a double boiler. Serve with rounds of toast.

Antipasto

12 thin slices of lean salami
6 slices tomato marinated in French Dressing
12 ripe olives
2 hard-cooked eggs
6 pickled artichoke hearts
2 sliced pickled beets

1 Combine ingredients and arrange on individual plates.

Sole and Salmon Rolls with Piquant Sauce

6 sole fillets
6 salmon slices, very thin
butter
1 oz can tomato sauce
4 oz tomato juice
2 tablespoons mayonnaise
juice of 1 lemon
2 oz butter or margarine

1 When buying fish ask dealer to roll sole around salmon.
2 Secure each roll with a toothpick.
3 Dot with plenty of butter.
4 Place rolls in a buttered baking dish.
5 Place in a pre-heated oven and bake at 350°F for 15 minutes without sauce.
6 Combine tomato sauce, tomato juice, mayonnaise, lemon juice and butter. Cook for at least 30 minutes.
7 Pour sauce over fish.
8 Bake in a pre-heated oven at 350°F for 45 minutes.
9 Add more butter or margarine, if desired.

Orange-Cranberry Mold

1 packet orange gelatin
1 cup hot water
1 can whole cranberries
½ cup sour cream
¼-½ cup nuts

1 Dissolve gelatin in hot water.
2 Add cranberries and juice.
3 Add sour cream and beat slightly with egg beater.
4 Add nuts.
5 Put in a greased mold and chill.

Cauliflower Pimiento Sauce

2 tablespoons flour
½ teaspoon salt
pepper
2 tablespoons butter, melted
1 cup hot milk
4 tablespoons pimiento purée
1 head cooked cauliflower
minced parsley

1 Blend flour, salt and pepper with melted butter.
2 Gradually pour on the milk.

3 Cook until creamy, stirring constantly.
4 Add pimiento purée (pimientos forced through a sieve or puréed in a blender).
5 Pour over cauliflower, sprinkle with parsley and serve.

Stuffed Zucchini

8 small zucchini
1 lb spinach
1 small onion, finely chopped
butter
1 cup Parmesan cheese
4 eggs, beaten
2 tablespoons olive oil
$\frac{1}{8}$ teaspoon salt
$\frac{1}{8}$ teaspoon pepper

1 Steam zucchini until tender.
2 Split and scoop out center.
3 Cook spinach in as little water as possible, season and chop finely.
4 Sauté onion in butter and add.
5 Beat eggs, mix with all the other ingredients, including the chopped centers of zucchini.
6 Stuff shells and bake for 25 minutes in a pre-heated oven at 400°F.

Divine Pie

4 eggs, separated
$\frac{1}{4}$ teaspoon cream of tartar
$1\frac{1}{2}$ cups sugar
3 tablespoons lemon juice
grated rind of 1 lemon
1 pint whipping cream

1 Beat egg whites until stiff.
2 Add cream of tartar when whites are foamy. Add 1 cup of sugar gradually (the remaining $\frac{1}{2}$ cup of sugar is to be used for the filling).
3 Line a greased pie plate with this mixture.
4 Spoon in the mixture so that it will be higher around the edges than the center.
5 Bake in a pre-heated oven at not more than 275°F for 1 hour.
6 Cool.
7 Place egg yolks in a double boiler over hot water. Add rest of sugar, lemon juice and $\frac{1}{8}$ lemon rind.
8 Stir for about 5 minutes or until mixture thickens. When cold, fold in 1 cup whipped cream.
9 Fill meringue shell with filling.
10 Spoon remaining whipped cream on top and sprinkle with remaining lemon rind. (Additional lemon rind may be used.)

Stuffed Breast of Veal (see page 150-1)

DINNER

Menu
No.6

Serves 4

Vegetable Bouillon

Chopped Chicken Livers
and/or
Beef in Wine and Herbs

Bean Salad

Vegetable Soufflé
and/or
Sweet Potato Bake

Strawberry Sherbet

Butter Cookies

Coffee or Tea

Tante Gussie's Gefilte Fish (see page 153)

Vegetable Bouillon

1 small head cabbage
1 medium onion
3 small carrots
1 stalk celery
2 quarts cold water
1 small can tomatoes
1 bunch parsley
1 bunch watercress

1 Dice cabbage and slice onion, carrots and celery, cover with water and boil for $2\frac{1}{2}$ hours over a medium heat.
2 Add tomatoes, parsley and watercress. Boil for 30 minutes longer.
3 Strain and serve as bouillon.

Chopped Chicken Livers

$\frac{1}{4}$ cup salad oil
$\frac{1}{2}$ cup diced onion
1 lb chicken livers, broiled
1 hard-cooked egg
$\frac{1}{2}$ teaspoon salt
$\frac{1}{4}$ teaspoon pepper
crisp lettuce leaves

Garnish
sliced tomato
radishes

1 Heat oil in a heavy skillet.
2 Add onion and sauté for about 5 minutes or until transparent.
3 Allow to cool.
4 Grind or chop together livers, egg and the entire contents of the skillet.
5 Stir in salt and pepper.
6 Chill until ready to serve.
7 Serve on lettuce leaves garnished with sliced tomato and red radishes.

Beef in Wine and Herbs

2 lb stew beef, cut into 2 inch cubes
Italian Dressing
1 teaspoon salt
$\frac{1}{2}$ teaspoon freshly ground pepper
1 cup red wine
2 bay leaves
1 tablespoon oil
$1\frac{1}{2}$ cups beef stock
$\frac{1}{2}$ teaspoon parsley
$\frac{1}{4}$ teaspoon thyme
$\frac{1}{4}$ teaspoon oregano
$\frac{1}{4}$ teaspoon basil
8 cloves
1 small can baby peas
1 small can French-style carrots
1 small can boiled onions

1 Place meat in a large bowl and add Italian dressing to cover salt, pepper, wine and bay leaves.
2 Marinate in the refrigerator for several hours, preferably overnight.
3 Remove meat, dry thoroughly, reserve marinade.
4 In a casserole, heat oil, add meat and brown on all sides.
5 Combine the reserved marinade, stock, herbs and spices. Simmer for 10 minutes.
6 Combine with meat, cover and simmer for $2\frac{1}{2}$-3 hours or until tender.
7 Add water, if necessary.
8 Add vegetables and cook until heated.
9 Remove cloves and bay leaves before serving.

Bean Salad

8 oz can green beans
8 oz can wax beans
8 oz can Italian beans
$\frac{1}{2}$ lb can red kidney beans
$\frac{1}{4}$ cup of minced onion
$\frac{1}{4}$ cup salad oil

¼ cup cider vinegar
¼ cup sugar
½ teaspoon salt

1 Combine beans, drain well, pour cold water over them, and drain again.
2 Place beans in a bowl and add onion.
3 Mix oil and vinegar with sugar and salt.
4 Pour over beans and toss well.
5 Refrigerate covered.
6 Serve on a lettuce leaf.

Vegetable Soufflé

1 turnip
2 carrots
2 parsnips
1 large onion
¼ cup margarine
¼ cup flour
vegetable juices
3 eggs, separated
⅛ teaspoon salt
⅛ teaspoon pepper

1 Dice vegetables finely and cook in water till soft.
2 Make a sauce with margarine, flour and juice in which vegetables were cooked.
3 Pureé the vegetables in a blender.
4 Beat egg yolks until smooth and add to 1 cup of vegetable purée.
5 Beat egg whites until stiff.
6 Add to purée mixture.
7 Combine mixture with white sauce.
8 Oil a 1 quart baking dish and put mixture into it.
9 Bake in a pre-heated oven at 325°F for 25 minutes or until cooked.
10 Serve hot.

Sweet Potato Bake

1 lb can whole sweet potatoes, drained
salt
½ cup brown sugar

1 tablespoon cornstarch
¼ teaspoon salt
1 cup orange juice
2 tablespoons dry sherry
walnut halves or chopped walnuts

1 Arrange sweet potatoes in a shallow baking dish.
2 Sprinkle lightly with salt.
3 In a saucepan mix brown sugar, cornstarch and salt.
4 Blend in orange juice.
5 Cook and stir over a high heat until mixture is boiling.
6 Add remaining ingredients and pour over potatoes.
7 Bake, uncovered, in a pre-heated oven at 350°F for 25-30 minutes or until potatoes are well glazed.

Strawberry Sherbet

1 cup sugar
½ cup water
½ cup crushed strawberries
¼ cup lemon and orange juice mixed
½ cup water
2 egg whites, stiffly beaten

1 Boil sugar and ½ cup water for 5 minutes.
2 Cool.
3 Add crushed strawberries, fruit juice and remaining water.
4 Beat mixture into stiffly beaten egg whites.
5 Chill in an ice cube tray or shallow glass baking dish.
6 When firm, place in a bowl and beat until smooth.
7 Re-freeze and repeat until mixture is as smooth as ice cream.
8 Serve in a sherbet glass with Butter Cookies.

Butter Cookies

1½ cups flour
⅛ teaspoon salt
¼ teaspoon baking powder
¼ lb margarine
½ cup sugar
1 egg yolk
½ teaspoon vanilla
1 tablespoon whiskey

Garnish
1 egg white
chopped nuts

1 Sift flour, salt and baking powder.
2 Combine all ingredients in a bowl and mix by hand.
3 Divide into three balls and make rolls about 1½ inches in diameter.
4 Refrigerate overnight.
5 Slice to desired thickness or roll out and cut with a cookie cutter.
6 Beat egg white lightly.
7 Brush tops of cookies with egg white and sprinkle with chopped nuts.
8 Bake on ungreased cookie sheets for about 15 minutes in a pre-heated oven at 375°F.

DINNER

Menu

No.7

Serves 6

Cabbage Borscht

Chicken and Meatball Fricassee
and/or
Stuffed Breast of Veal

Garden Salad

Beet Mold
and/or
Squash on the Half-Shell

Carrot Cake

Coffee or Tea

Cabbage Borscht

1 small onion
2½ lb cabbage
2 tablespoons vegetable oil
¼ teaspoon salt
2 lb flanken and bones
2½ cups tomatoes
1 can tomato soup
6 cups water
juice of 1 lemon
1 teaspoon sugar

1 Grate onion and cabbage, season, and brown with meat slowly for about 20 minutes in oil.
2 Stir occasionally.
3 Add tomatoes, tomato soup, water and lemon juice.
4 Add sugar when soup is cooked.
5 Cover and simmer for about 2½ hours.

Chicken and Meatball Fricassee

½ lb ground beef
1 egg, beaten
4 tablespoons dried breadcrumbs
¼ teaspoon onion powder
¼ teaspoon garlic powder
⅛ teaspoon ground black pepper
1 teaspoon soy sauce
3 tablespoons peanut oil
1 clove garlic, crushed
2 lb chicken, cut up
¼ teaspoon salt
⅛ teaspoon pepper
⅛ teaspoon paprika
1 tablespoon soy sauce
1 small bunch green onions, cut up

1 Combine beef, egg, breadcrumbs, onion powder, garlic powder, pepper and soy sauce.
2 Blend well and shape into ¾ inch balls.
3 Brown on all sides beneath a moderately hot broiler.

4 Heat oil in a skillet and sauté garlic until lightly browned and add chicken pieces.
5 While chicken is browning season with salt, pepper and paprika.
6 Add soy sauce and green onions.
7 Cover skillet and simmer gently until chicken is tender.
8 If skillet becomes too dry add some chicken bouillon, a little at a time, as required.
9 Add meatballs to skillet, heat thoroughly and serve.

Stuffed Breast of Veal

Stuffing
1 large onion, minced
1 green pepper, diced
2 stalks celery, diced
2 tablespoons oil
5 slices bread
1 teaspoon salt
⅛ teaspoon pepper
2 eggs

Breast of veal
3-4 lb veal with pocket
1 teaspoon salt
¼ teaspoon pepper
¼ teaspoon celery salt
1 garlic clove, minced, OR ¼ teaspoon garlic salt
½ cup water
¼ cup matzo meal
2 tablespoons chicken fat

1 Sauté stuffing vegetables in oil.
2 Soak bread in water.
3 Squeeze out water, and retain only the bread pulp.
4 Combine all stuffing ingredients and mix well.
5 Sprinkle inside of pocket of veal thoroughly with salt, pepper, celery salt and garlic.
6 Stuff the pocket with the stuffing.
7 Sew up pocket and place veal in a roasting pan.

8 Add water, matzo meal and chicken fat.
9 Cover and roast in a pre-heated oven at 350°F, allowing 20 minutes cooking per pound.
10 Baste several times while baking.

Garden Salad

2 cucumbers
2 large tomatoes
1 sweet onion
5-6 sprigs parsley, chopped
3 tablespoons French Dressing

1 Into a flat glass dish slice a layer of fresh cucumber, then a layer of tomatoes, then thin slices of onion.
2 Sprinkle parsley over the top.
3 Sprinkle French dressing over the salad.
4 Stand for an hour before serving.

Beet Mold

1 packet lemon gelatin
1 cup hot water
$\frac{3}{4}$ cup beet juice
2 tablespoons vinegar
$\frac{1}{2}$ cup diced beets
$\frac{1}{2}$ cup diced celery
2 tablespoons onion juice
2 tablespoons horseradish

1 Dissolve gelatin in water.
2 Add beet juice, vinegar and rest of ingredients.
3 Place in a lightly oiled ring mold and chill until firm.
4 Dip mold in warm water for a few seconds. Invert onto a large platter so beet mold comes out cleanly.

Squash on the Half-Shell

3 medium acorn squash
3 tablespoons margarine
3 teaspoons corn syrup
1 teaspoon salt
$\frac{1}{8}$ teaspoon pepper

1 Scrub squash.
2 Cut in half lengthwise.
3 Remove seeds and stringy parts.
4 Brush cut surface of each half with 2 tablespoons margarine.
5 Arrange halves, cut side down, in a shallow baking pan.
6 Bake in a pre-heated oven at 400°F for 30 minutes.
7 Turn cut side up, brush halves with corn syrup, remaining margarine, salt and pepper.
8 Continue baking for 20-30 minutes or until tender.

Carrot Cake

$\frac{1}{4}$ lb margarine
$1\frac{1}{4}$ cups sugar
4 eggs
$2\frac{1}{2}$ cups cake flour
pinch salt
2 teaspoons baking powder
$\frac{1}{2}$ teaspoon soda bicarbonate
1 cup grated fresh carrot
$1\frac{1}{2}$ cups warm water
1 cup walnuts
$\frac{1}{2}$ cup chopped raisins
1 oz mixed candied fruit

1 Cream margarine.
2 Blend in sugar.
3 Add eggs.
4 Combine flour, salt, baking powder and soda and sift.
5 Add dry mixture to butter mixture.
6 Press water out of carrots, using a cheese cloth.
7 Add carrots and other ingredients.
8 Place in a greased cake tin and bake in a pre-heated oven at 350°F for 50-60 minutes.

DINNER

Menu

No.8

Serves 8

Jellied Tomato Consommé

Mushroom Strudel
and/or
Tante Gussie's Gefilte Fish

Cabbage and Pineapple Salad

Cauliflower au Gratin
and/or
Mock Wild Rice Ring

Cheese Cake

Coffee or Tea

Jellied Tomato Consommé

1 can consommé
2 cups tomato juice
⅛ teaspoon salt
⅛ teaspoon pepper
1 tablespoon gelatin
¼ cup cold water

Garnish
lemon slices

1 Mix consommé and tomato juice and season to taste.
2 Heat.
3 Soak gelatin for 5 minutes in cold water.
4 Add to hot mixture, stirring until dissolved.
5 Chill until thickened.
6 Garnish with lemon slices.

Mushroom Strudel

6 tablespoons butter or margarine
1 lb mushrooms, finely chopped
shallots or scallions to taste
2 tablespoons Madeira wine
salt and freshly ground pepper to taste
½ teaspoon tarragon
½ cup sour cream
1 packet strudel leaves
½ cup melted butter
1 cup fine dry breadcrumbs

1 Preheat oven to 375°F.
2 Melt butter.
3 Add mushrooms, shallots, wine, salt, pepper and tarragon.
4 Cook, stirring occasionally until most of liquid has evaporated.
5 Let mixture cool slightly.
6 Stir in sour cream.
7 Brush strudel leaves with melted butter and sprinkle with breadcrumbs.
8 Form sausage shape with the mixture at the bottom of the strudel leaf; fold over and roll.

9 Brush with butter.
10 On buttered baking sheet cut into 1½ inch servings.
11 Bake 15-20 minutes, until crisp and brown.

Tante Gussie's Gefilte Fish

fish bones, heads and skin
5 medium onions
cold water
3 lb pike and white fish
2 eggs
¼ cup matzo meal
2 teaspoons salt
½ teaspoon pepper
1 teaspoon sugar
3 oz cold water

1 Place fish bones, heads and skin in the bottom of a heavy pot.
2 Slice 4 onions over these.
3 Cover with cold water and bring to the boil.
4 Grind fish with 1 onion.
5 Add eggs, matzo meal, salt, pepper, sugar and water to fish mixture.
6 It is best to mix the ingredients thoroughly by hand.
7 Wet hands in cold water and form fish into balls or patties.
8 Drop balls into boiling fish soup.
9 Cover and boil for about 2½-3 hours. (Boil; do not simmer.)
10 When cooked, remove fish balls from pot with a slotted spoon and place on a platter.
11 Strain soup and pour over the fish balls.

Cabbage and Pineapple Salad

2 cups finely shredded white cabbage
1 cup shredded pineapple
juice of ½ lemon

salt
pepper
sugar
mayonnaise

1 Combine cabbage and drained pineapple.
2 Add lemon juice and salt, pepper and sugar to taste.
3 Moisten with mayonnaise and chill.
4 Serve in mounds on pineapple slices, on lettuce leaves, or in a hollowed savoy cabbage.

Cauliflower au Gratin

1 large head cauliflower (about 2 lb)
boiling water
$\frac{1}{8}$ teaspoon salt

Sauce
$\frac{1}{4}$ cup finely chopped onion
4 tablespoons butter or margarine
2 tablespoons flour
$\frac{1}{2}$ teaspoon salt
$\frac{1}{8}$ teaspoon pepper
1$\frac{1}{2}$ cups milk
$\frac{1}{4}$ cup dry breadcrumbs
2 tablespoons grated Parmesan cheese

1 Wash cauliflower thoroughly; cut into flowerets.
2 Cover and cook, in 1 inch salted boiling water for 10-15 minutes, or until just tender.
3 Drain well.
4 Preheat oven to 350°F.
5 Sauté onion in 2 tablespoons hot butter for about 5 minutes until golden.
6 Remove from heat; stir in flour, salt and pepper until well blended.
7 Gradually stir in milk; bring to the boil, stirring constantly.
8 Reduce heat and simmer for 1 minute.
9 Place cauliflower in 1$\frac{1}{2}$ quart casserole.
10 Pour sauce over cauliflower.
11 In a small skillet, melt 2 tablespoons butter.

12 Stir in breadcrumbs and cheese.
13 Sprinkle over cauliflower.
14 Bake uncovered in a pre-heated oven at 350°F for 20-25 minutes, or until sauce is bubbly and top is golden.

Mock Wild Rice Ring

1 cup rice
$\frac{3}{4}$ lb mushrooms
2 tablespoons butter
1 small onion
$\frac{1}{4}$ teaspoon salt
$\frac{1}{8}$ teaspoon pepper

1 Cook rice according to instructions on packet.
2 Grind mushrooms and sauté in butter with chopped onion, salt and pepper.
3 Add to cooked rice and simmer for 15 minutes.
4 Put mixture in a buttered ring mold. Set mold in a pan of boiling water and bake in a pre-heated oven at 350°F for 45 minutes.

Cheese Cake

2 cups Zwieback crumbs
2 tablespoons margarine or butter
2 tablespoons sugar
4 eggs, separated
1 cup cream
1 lb cream cheese
1 cup sugar
2 tablespoons flour
$\frac{1}{8}$ teaspoon salt
1 teaspoon vanilla extract

Garnish
fresh strawberries

1 Mix crumbs with margarine or butter and sugar.

2 In a springform cake pan press batter into an even layer across the bottom and half way up the sides.

3 Beat egg yolks to a creamy yellow.

4 Add remaining ingredients and mix well.

5 Fold in stiffly beaten egg whites.

6 Pour into the springform.

7 Bake in a pre-heated oven at 325°F for 1 hour or until cake is firm and browned.

8 Turn off the oven and leave cake there for 1 hour to cool.

9 Garnish with a decoration of strawberries or other fruit of your choice.

DINNER

Menu

No.9

Serves 6

Petite Marmite
and/or
Hummus

Lamb or Beef Kebabs

Molded Apple Cider Salad

Cranberry Sauce

Glazed Sweet Potatoes
and/or
Asparagus Polonaise

Honey Cake

Coffee or Tea

Petite Marmite

1 onion, sliced
margarine
4 cups consommé
1 leek, diced
4 tablespoons chopped carrots
$\frac{1}{2}$ small cabbage, chopped
2 cloves garlic, crushed
1 cup diced roast chicken
$\frac{1}{4}$ teaspoon salt
Tabasco sauce to taste

1 Sauté onion in a little margarine.
2 Heat consommé; add vegetables and garlic and cook until tender.
3 Add chicken and seasonings.
4 Serve in individual earthenware pots, with a piece of toasted French bread to cover the top.

Hummus

$\frac{1}{2}$ lb chick peas
water
$\frac{1}{2}$ cup oil (preferably sesame oil)
2-3 cloves garlic, pounded
$\frac{1}{4}$ teaspoon salt
juice of 1 lemon
ground red pepper (optional)

1 Soak chick peas in water overnight.
2 Remove skins and cook for 4 hours until soft.
3 Mash.
4 Blend in oil, garlic, salt and lemon juice.
5 Mix together and sprinkle with red pepper.
6 Spread on thinly sliced bread or light toast and serve.

Lamb or Beef Kebabs

$\frac{3}{4}$ cup pineapple juice from can
2 tablespoons soy sauce
2 tablespoons lemon juice
1 garlic clove, minced
3 lb lamb or beef, cut in 2 inch cubes
12 small white onions
green pepper, cut in bite-size pieces
2 cups canned pineapple chunks, drained
12 cherry tomatoes

1 Combine pineapple juice, soy sauce, lemon juice and garlic.
2 Marinate lamb cubes in mixture at room temperature for about 6 hours.
3 Thread lamb on skewers with onions and green pepper.
4 Broil or grill for about 15-20 minutes.
5 Thread pineapple and tomatoes on separate skewers and broil for about 10 minutes.

Molded Apple Cider Salad

1 tablespoon gelatin
$\frac{1}{4}$ cup cold water
2 cups apple cider
1 cup apple sauce, sweetened and seasoned

1 Soak gelatin in cold water for 5 minutes.
2 Heat cider to boiling point, then remove from heat.
3 Add gelatin and stir until dissolved.
4 Cool, stir in apple sauce, pour into a ring mold and chill.
5 Turn out and serve with any fruit salad combination.
Note: Celery Seed Dressing is delicious with this salad. (See page 26.)

Cranberry Sauce

2 cups sugar
1 cup water
1 lb fresh cranberries
$\frac{1}{4}$ cup pineapple preserves
juice and rind of 1 lemon
$\frac{1}{2}$ cup blanched almonds, slivered

1 Put sugar and water in a saucepan and bring to the boil.
2 Cook for 5 minutes.
3 Add cranberries and cook until skins pop open.
4 Stir in preserves and lemon juice and rind.
5 Cool.
6 Stir in almonds.
7 Chill and serve.

Glazed Sweet Potatoes

$\frac{1}{2}$ cup brown sugar
$\frac{1}{3}$ cup water
1 tablespoon margarine
$\frac{1}{4}$ teaspoon salt
1 lb 7 oz can sweet potatoes

1 Combine all ingredients except potatoes in a frying pan and simmer for 5 minutes.
2 Add whole potatoes and simmer for 10 minutes.
3 Turn potatoes often to glaze well.

Asparagus Polonaise

2 lb fresh asparagus
6 tablespoons margarine
$\frac{1}{3}$ cup breadcrumbs
1 tablespoon lemon juice
2 tablespoons chopped parsley
1 hard-cooked egg yolk, sieved
$\frac{1}{4}$ teaspoon salt
$\frac{1}{8}$ teaspoon pepper

1 Wash and trim asparagus.
2 Cook until barely tender.
3 Place drained asparagus in a serving dish and keep warm.
4 In a saucepan heat the margarine until it just starts to color.
5 Add remaining ingredients and sauté until lightly browned.
6 Sprinkle over asparagus.
7 Serve.

Honey Cake

1 cup sugar
$\frac{1}{2}$ cup soft shortening
3 eggs
1 lb honey
3 cups flour
1 teaspoon baking powder
1 teaspoon baking soda
$\frac{1}{8}$ teaspoon salt
1 teaspoon cinnamon
1 teaspoon ground cloves
$\frac{1}{2}$ teaspoon ground ginger
1 teaspoon nutmeg
1 teaspoon allspice
1 cup strong tea

1 Cream sugar and shortening.
2 Add eggs, one at a time, beating well after each addition.
3 Add honey.
4 Sift dry ingredients together. Add tea and mix well.
5 Grease 9 inch x 13 inch pan, line with waxed paper and grease paper.
6 Pour in batter and bake in a pre-heated oven at 325°F for 30 minutes.
7 Cool cake before you cut it.

DINNER

No.10

Serves 6

Vegetable Soup

Sweet and Sour Cabbage Rolls
and/or
Pot Roast

Jellied Apricot Salad

Marinated Vegetables
and/or
Boiled Onions

Old-Fashioned Apple Pie

Coffee or Tea

Vegetable Soup

1 quart soup stock
1 tablespoon uncooked rice
$\frac{1}{4}$ cup diced carrots
$\frac{1}{4}$ cup diced celery
$\frac{1}{4}$ cup diced potatoes
$\frac{1}{8}$ cup dried navy beans
1 large can tomatoes
$\frac{1}{4}$ cup fresh lima beans
2 oz okra, sliced
$\frac{1}{2}$ cup corn kernels
$\frac{1}{2}$ teaspoon sugar
$\frac{1}{4}$ teaspoon salt
$\frac{1}{8}$ teaspoon pepper
$\frac{1}{4}$ tablespoon minced parsley

1 Bring soup stock to the boil; add rice and cook for 10-15 minutes.
2 Add vegetables and seasonings.
3 Cook for about 35-40 minutes or until vegetables are tender.
4 Add parsley before serving.

Sweet and Sour Cabbage Rolls

$1\frac{1}{2}$ lb lean chopped meat
$\frac{1}{4}$ cup uncooked rice
$\frac{1}{4}$ cup water
1 large head of cabbage, with large outer leaves
$\frac{1}{4}$ teaspoon salt
$\frac{1}{8}$ teaspoon freshly ground pepper

Sauce
6 small ginger snaps
$\frac{1}{2}$ cup brown sugar
1 cup stock or canned bouillon
$\frac{1}{4}$ cup cider vinegar
$\frac{1}{2}$ cup raisins
1 lemon, sliced thinly

1 Mix meat, rice and water.
2 Parboil cabbage for at least 5 minutes, until leaves are tender and pliable.

3 Separate leaves, and in the center of each leaf put a small patty of raw meat. Season with salt and pepper.
4 Fold each leaf over into an envelope and place in layers in a deep saucepan.
5 Combine ginger snaps, brown sugar, stock and vinegar.
6 Heat in a saucepan and cook until sauce has thickened.
7 Add raisins and sliced lemon and simmer over a low heat until fruits are tender and slightly glazed.
8 If sauce gets too thick, add extra liquid.
9 Pour sauce over cabbage rolls and simmer gently for $1-1\frac{1}{2}$ hours or until well cooked.
10 If cooked ahead of serving time, the cabbage rolls and sauce can be put into a casserole and reheated in the oven. This thickens the sauce and adds a slightly crusty finish.

Pot Roast

$\frac{1}{4}$ cup oil
3 lb chuck roast
1 carrot
1 stalk celery, chopped
1 large onion, chopped
2 cloves garlic, minced
2 bay leaves
salt and pepper
4 oz can mushrooms
1 cup red wine or rosé
8 oz can tomato paste
2 cups beef broth
2 large potatoes, sliced (optional)

1 Heat oil.
2 Brown roast on all sides.
3 Add carrot, celery, onion and garlic and sauté until onion is golden.

(Continued on page 163)

Old Fashioned Apple Pie (see page 163-4)

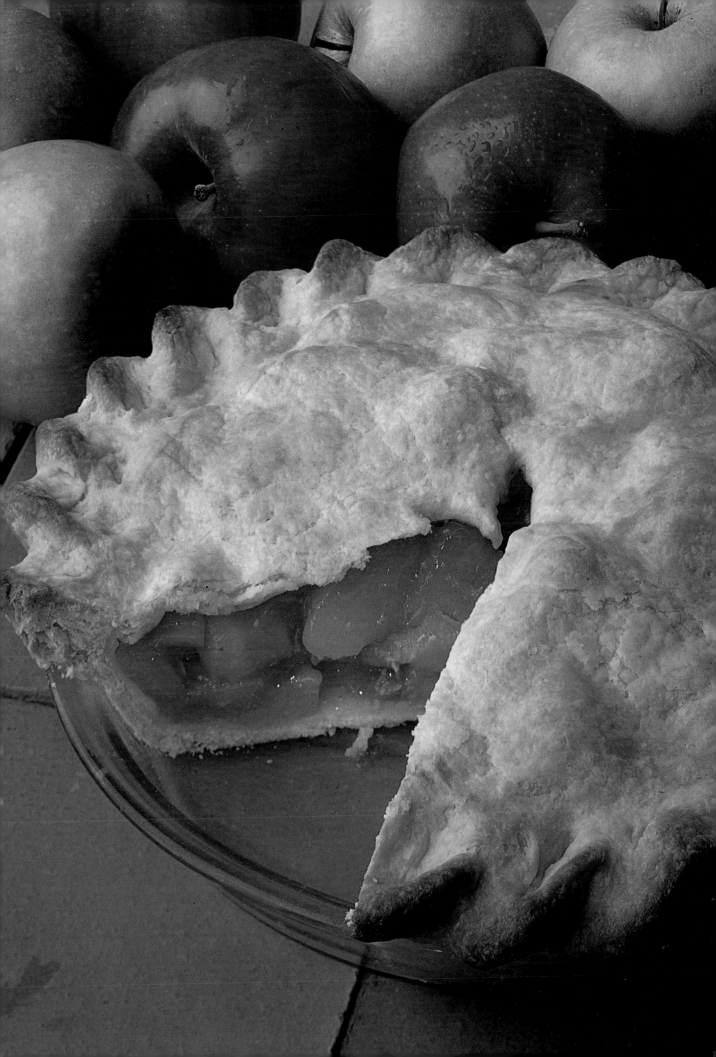

4 Add bay leaves, mushrooms, salt and pepper.
5 Cook over a low heat for 5 minutes.
6 Add wine, tomato paste and beef broth.
7 Cover and bring to the boil.
8 Continue cooking over a low heat for about 2½ hours or until tender, stirring occasionally.
9 Add more broth if necessary.
10 If desired, sliced potatoes may be added to the meat during the last hour of cooking.

Jellied Apricot Salad

1 large can whole peeled apricots
⅓ cup peanut butter
¼ cup chopped walnuts
¼ cup chopped dates
juice of 1 lemon
1 packet lemon gelatin
2 cups hot water.

1 Remove the pits from drained apricots.
2 Combine peanut butter, chopped nuts and chopped dates with lemon juice and mix well.
3 Fill the cavity of each apricot with a spoonful of this mixture, pressing the halves together so that the fruit looks whole.
4 Put one filled apricot in individual molds or muffin tins.
5 Dissolve lemon gelatin in hot water and chill until almost set.
6 Pour lemon gelatin in molds and chill.

Marinated Vegetables

1 small head cauliflower
1 green pepper, cut into ½ inch pieces
½ cup sliced fresh carrot
½ cup sliced fresh mushroom
½ cup sliced celery

Komyss Brot (see page 170)

½ cup sliced stuffed olives
¼ cup wine vinegar
¼ cup olive oil
¼ cup fresh lemon juice
¼ cup water
2 tablespoons sugar
1 teaspoon salt
½ teaspoon crumbled basil leaves
2 bay leaves

1 Combine all ingredients in large saucepan and cook for 5 minutes.
2 Let mixture cool, and refrigerate overnight before serving.
Note: Marinated Vegetables will last for several weeks and taste better with age.

Boiled Onions

12 small white onions
1½ cups boiling water
3 tablespoons margarine
1 tablespoon vinegar

1 Put onions in rapidly boiling salted water.
2 Boil until tender. Drain.
3 Melt several tablespoons margarine with 1 tablespoon vinegar and pour over onions.
4 Stir and cook for a few minutes.

Old-Fashioned Apple Pie

7 tart apples
juice of ½ lemon
1 cup sugar
3 tablespoons flour
¾ teaspoon nutmeg

Pastry
2 cups sifted flour
1 teaspoon salt
⅔ cup shortening
4 tablespoons cold water

1 Pare, core and slice apples; pour lemon juice over apples.
2 Mix sugar, flour and nutmeg, and pour over apples. Set aside.
3 Sift pastry flour and salt. Work in $\frac{1}{3}$ cup shortening.
4 Cut in second $\frac{1}{3}$ cup of shortening with a knife. Add water and mix quickly.
5 Roll dough into a thin sheet and cover bottom and sides of a greased 9-inch pie pan. Retain some dough for top.
6 Put apple mixture into pan.
7 Cover with balance of rolled-out dough.
8 With knife pierce dough cover in 6 places.
9 Bake in a pre-heated oven at 475°F for 15 minutes, then reduce heat to 350°F and cook for about $1\frac{1}{2}$ hours.
10 Cool before serving.

DINNER

No. 11

Serves 6

Onion Soup
and/or
Mushroom Cheese Puffs

Codfish Supreme

Avocado Ring

Broccoli Casserole
and/or
Corn Fritters

Marble Cake

Coffee or Tea

Onion Soup

5 large onions
6 tablespoons oil
1½ quarts hot water
4 bouillon cubes
6 rounds bread, crusts trimmed
8 oz Gruyére cheese, grated
freshly ground pepper

1 Cut onions in half, slice paper thin.
2 Heat oil and sauté onions.
3 Add water and bouillon cubes.
4 Bring to the boil and simmer for 10 minutes.
5 Toast bread rounds in the oven, then put one on the bottom of each of 6 ovenproof bowls.
6 Gently ladle soup into bowls so that bread remains on bottom.
7 Garnish generously with cheese and pepper.
8 Put under broiler until cheese browns.

Mushroom Cheese Puffs

½ lb mushroom caps
2 tablespoons butter
6 oz soft cream cheese
1 egg yolk, beaten
⅛ teaspoon minced onion
bread rounds

1 Sauté mushroom caps in butter.
2 Blend cream cheese, egg yolk and onion together.
3 Toast bread rounds (as many as there are mushrooms) under broiler on one side.
4 Place dab of cheese mixture on untoasted sides.
5 Top with mushroom caps, round side down.
6 Cover with cheese mixture.
7 Broil until puffy and slightly brown.
Note: If using canned mushrooms, don't sauté.

Codfish Supreme

6 pieces codfish, about ½-¾ inch thick
¾ cup mayonnaise
¾ cup sour cream

1 Preheat broiler.
2 Wash fish under cold running water and dry in paper toweling.
3 Place fish in pan.
4 Blend mayonnaise and sour cream and spread on top of fish.
5 Broil for 20-30 minutes.
6 Fish should be brown and bubbly on top and white and flaky inside when cooked.

Avocado Ring

1 packet lemon gelatin
1 cup boiling water
1 cup sour cream
1 cup mayonnaise
1 cup mashed avocado

1 Dissolve gelatin in boiling water.
2 Cool.
3 Add sour cream, mayonnaise and avocado.
4 Turn into mold that has been rinsed in cold water.

Broccoli Casserole

2 packets frozen broccoli
2 tablespoons butter or margarine
⅛ teaspoon nutmeg
¼ teaspoon salt
⅛ teaspoon freshly ground pepper
½ cup finely grated Swiss cheese
½ cup finely grated Parmesan cheese

1 Boil broccoli in large amount of salted water until just tender.
2 Put in blender with ½ inch water in bottom for each batch you purée.
3 Preheat oven to 350°F.
4 Melt tablespoons butter or margarine in saucepan.
5 Add broccoli purée and season with nutmeg, salt and pepper.
6 Put in a large greased casserole and sprinkle top with a mixture of cheeses.
7 Bake in the oven for 20 minutes or until brown.

Corn Fritters

1 cup grated fresh or canned corn
⅔ cup flour
½ teaspoon baking powder
½ teaspoon salt
dash paprika
1 egg

1 Chop corn, drain, add dry ingredients mixed and sifted.
2 Add egg yolk beaten until thick.
3 Fold in egg white beaten until stiff.
4 Drop spoonfuls into pan and fry in deep fat at 370°F.
5 Drain on paper towels.

Marble Cake

¼ pound butter or margarine
2 cups sugar
4 eggs, separated
2 cups flour
2 teaspoons baking powder
½ cup milk
1 teaspoon vanilla
2 oz bitter chocolate
⅓ cup milk

1 Cream butter or margarine and sugar.
2 Add egg yolks.
3 Sift flour and baking powder together and add to creamed mixture with ½ cup milk.
4 Add vanilla.
5 Fold in stiffly beaten egg whites.
6 Melt chocolate in the top of a double boiler and add ⅓ cup milk.
7 Cool slightly.
8 Add 4 heaped tablespoons of the white batter.
9 Pour half of the white batter into a well-greased 12 inch x 8 inch baking pan.
10 Cover with chocolate batter.
11 Pour remaining white batter over this.
12 Bake in a pre-heated oven at 350°F for about 50-60 minutes.
13 Serve with fresh or canned pears, peaches, cherries, grapes, plums or pineapple.

DINNER

Menu

No. 12

Serves 4

Chicken Gumbo

Deviled Roe
and/or
Herbed Veal with White Wine

Guacamole Salad

Braised Celery with Almonds
and/or
Fluffed Rice

Komyss Brot

Coffee or Tea

Chicken Gumbo

1 onion, finely chopped
4 tablespoons margarine
1 quart chicken stock
½ green pepper, finely chopped
1 cup cooked or canned okra
2 teaspoons salt
dash pepper
1-2 cups canned tomatoes
shredded chicken

1 Cook onion in margarine for 5 minutes, stirring constantly.
2 Add to stock with remaining ingredients
3 Bring to the boil and simmer for 40 minutes.

Deviled Roe

7-8 pieces fish roe, fresh or canned
2 tablespoons margarine, melted
⅔ teaspoon dry mustard
2½ teaspoons Worcestershire sauce
⅛ teaspoon salt
12 slices toast

Garnish
lemon slices

1 Drain fish roe.
2 Mix margarine, mustard, Worcestershire sauce and salt. Roll fish in mixture.
3 Mash well.
4 Spread on toast.
5 Place in a pre-heated oven at 425°F for about 5 minutes.
6 Garnish with thin slices of lemon.

Herbed Veal with White Wine

3 tablespoons oil
1 clove garlic, cut in half
1¼ lb veal cutlets

¼ teaspoon salt
⅛ teaspoon pepper
⅛ teaspoon oregano
⅛ teaspoon rosemary
⅛ teaspoon marjoram
⅓ cup dry white wine

1 Heat oil in a large skillet and sauté garlic clove.
2 Remove garlic and discard.
3 Put in veal, a layer at a time.
4 As veal slices brown, dust with salt, pepper and herbs.
5 When veal is well browned on both sides, add wine, stirring with a wooden spoon to blend in all the pan scrapings.
6 Cover skillet and simmer gently for about 20 minutes.
7 Arrange veal slices on a warm platter and spoon pan juices over them.

Guacamole Salad

1 clove garlic
1 avocado
1 teaspoon lemon juice
1 onion, grated
1 small tomato, finely chopped
¼ teaspoon salt
1-2 drops Tabasco sauce
1 tomato, thinly sliced
lettuce leaf

1 Rub a bowl with garlic.
2 Mash avocado with lemon juice, grated onion, chopped tomato, salt and Tabasco sauce. Mix thoroughly.
3 Chill.
4 Pile the mixture on tomato slices and serve on a lettuce leaf.

Braised Celery with Almonds

2½ cups celery, cut diagonally in ½ inch strips
2 tablespoons chopped onion

1 tablespoon margarine
¼ can bouillon or consommé
¼ teaspoon salt
⅛ teaspoon pepper
¼ cup chopped, roasted, unblanched
   almonds

1 Slowly, sauté celery and onion in
   margarine until lightly browned.
2 Add consommé, salt and pepper.
3 Cover; cook until tender and liquid is
   absorbed.
4 When ready to serve, add chopped
   almonds.
Note: Braised Celery can also be baked in the
oven.

Fluffed Rice

2 quarts water
1 teaspoon salt
1 cup rice

1 Bring water and salt to the boil.
2 Slowly sprinkle rice into boiling water so
   the water keeps boiling.
3 Stir rice twice.
4 Reduce heat to low, cover pot partially
   and cook for 20 minutes.
5 Drain into colander and rinse under cold
   water.
6 Put rice in a covered dish and heat in the
   oven at 350°F for 20 minutes.
7 Serve in a warmed dish.

Komyss Brot

¼ lb margarine
1¾ cups sugar
6 eggs
juice and rind of 1 lemon
juice and rind of 1 orange
1 teaspoon vanilla
1 tablespoon brandy
⅛ teaspoon salt
4-4½ cups flour
4 teaspoons baking powder
22 broken walnuts or blanched almonds

1 Cream margarine, blend in sugar, and add
   one egg at a time, beating well.
2 Add juice of lemon and orange and a little
   rind of each. Add vanilla, brandy and
   salt.
3 Gradually add flour, sifted with baking
   powder.
4 Add nuts.
5 Drop a large piece of dough onto a baking
   sheet and shape with a spoon into a long
   loaf, about 1 inch high and 3 inches wide.
   Place loaves about 2 inches apart as loaves
   spread while baking.
6 Bake in a pre-heated oven at 350°F until
   light brown.
7 Cut crosswise into strips while still warm.
Note: Komyss Brot keeps indefinitely and
improves with age.

DINNER

No.13

Serves 6

Onion Soup
and/or
Herring Salad

Baked Steak

Apple Cranberry Mold

Roste Potatoes
and/or
Pan-Fried Pineapple

Steamed Date and Nut Pudding

Coffee or Tea

Onion Soup

3 cups thinly sliced onions
4 tablespoons margarine
6 cups strong chicken or beef broth

1 Sauté onions in margarine until brown.
2 Add broth and simmer for 20 minutes.
3 Season and serve with squares of crisp toast.

Herring Salad

3 herrings
2 apples
2 sticks celery, diced
½ onion, grated
½ pint sour cream substitute

Garnish
1 slice sweet, red onion

1 Bone and cut herrings into small pieces.
2 Peel, core and cut up apples into small pieces.
3 Mix all ingredients together.
4 Serve on lettuce and garnish with a slice of sweet red onion.

Baked Steak

1 London broil, at least 2 inches thick,
   OR 2-2½ lb piece shoulder steak
4 oz margarine
½ cup catsup
¼ cup Worcestershire Sauce
⅛ teaspoon garlic salt

1 Dot meat with margarine.
2 Combine catsup and Worcestershire sauce and pour over meat.
3 Sprinkle with garlic salt.
4 Bake in a pre-heated oven at 400°- 425°F for 30-45 minutes.
Note: Do not overcook; serve rare.

Apple Cranberry Mold

1 packet red gelatin
1¼ cups boiling water
2 cups whole cranberry sauce
1 cup diced apples
½ cup diced celery
¼ cup chopped nuts

1 Dissolve gelatin in hot water.
2 Add cranberry sauce.
3 Chill until partially set.
4 Add remaining ingredients.
5 Pour into a 4 cup mold.
6 Chill until firm.
7 To serve: dip mold in warm water up to rim. Turn mold upside down on a platter and tap to loosen. If unsuccessful, dip again.

Rosté Potatoes

3 large potatoes
2 onions
¼ teaspoon salt
⅛ teaspoon freshly ground pepper
½ cup shortening or margarine

1 Peel potatoes and grate on the large side of grater.
2 Grate onions, mix with potato and season with salt and pepper.
3 Drain all water from this mixture.
4 Melt shortening in a skillet; add potato mixture.
5 Cook over a medium to high heat.
6 Use a spatula to work mixture toward center from the sides to prevent it sticking.
7 As edges begin to brown, place large platter over skillet and turn potatoes onto it.
8 Slide potatoes back into skillet to brown other side.
9 Potatoes should be the shape of the skillet and brown crusted on both sides when cooked.
10 Cut into wedges and serve.

Pan-Fried Pineapple

1 medium pineapple, peeled, cored and
   sliced, OR 1 small can pineapple slices
½ cup flour
3 tablespoons margarine

1 Cut slices of pineapple in two.
2 Dip into flour and place in a hot frying
  pan with melted margarine.
3 Brown on one side, turn and brown the
  other side.
4 Serve with baked meat.

Steamed Date and Nut Pudding

4 eggs
½ cup granulated sugar
1 cup all-purpose flour
½ teaspoon salt
½ cup whole wheat flour
2 teaspoons baking powder
4 tablespoons chopped walnuts
10 dates, chopped
1 tablespoon shortening or margarine

1 Beat eggs and sugar together until light
  and fluffy.
2 Sift dry ingredients together, add nuts
  and dates and blend thoroughly.
3 Fold into sugar mixture.
4 Grease individual molds with tight fitting
  covers, with margarine.
5 Steam for 45-50 minutes.
6 Serve with Dessert Whip.

DINNER

No.14

Serves 6

Leek Soup
and/or
Calf's Foot Jelly

Veal with Olives

Pineapple and Cucumber Mold

Peas and Mushrooms
and/or
Baked Lettuce

Frosted Chocolate Cake

Coffee or Tea

Leek Soup

2 lb soup beef
soup bones
soup greens
2 medium potatoes
$\frac{1}{4}$ teaspoon salt
$\frac{1}{8}$ teaspoon pepper
$2\frac{1}{2}$ cups tomatoes
2 bay leaves
2-3 cloves
3 quarts cold water
10 leeks
1 tablespoon Kitchen Bouquet

1 Place meat, soup bones, greens, potatoes, salt and pepper, tomatoes, bay leaves and cloves in a soup pot with the water.
2 Cook until the meat is tender.
3 Tie the leeks together, add to the soup and cook until tender.
4 Remove leeks and cut them into small pieces.
5 Strain soup, rub all vegetables through a fine sieve or purée in a blender.
6 Return vegetables to the pot, add leeks and cook for 30 minutes. Add Kitchen Bouquet to soup just before serving.

Calf's Foot Jelly

3 calves' feet
3 large onions, chopped
3 cloves garlic, crushed
1 tablespoon salt
4 quarts water
3 egg yolks
$\frac{3}{4}$ cup vinegar
2 tablespoons sugar

1 Ask the butcher to chop the calves' feet into small pieces. Put calves' feet, onions, garlic, salt and water in a large pot.
2 Boil for $2\frac{1}{2}$ hours until there is approximately 2 quarts liquid left. Strain.
3 Cut the meat and gristle from the bones and grind or chop finely. Discard bones.

4 When soup is cool stir in egg yolks, vinegar and sugar.
5 Bring to the boil and then set aside for 10 minutes.
6 Combine the ground meat and soup. Mix thoroughly and pour into shallow dishes or platters to set.

Veal with Olives

2 lb veal, cut into $1\frac{1}{2}$ inch cubes
flour for dredging
salt
freshly ground pepper
3 tablespoons peanut oil
2 cups boiling water
1 clove garlic, minced
1 medium onion, sliced
1 teaspoon chopped rosemary
$\frac{1}{2}$ cup dry white wine
$\frac{1}{4}$ cup tomato sauce
1 cup beef stock
$\frac{3}{4}$ cup chopped black olives
$\frac{1}{2}$ cup chopped parsley

1 Preheat oven to 300° F.
2 Dredge veal with flour seasoned with salt and pepper.
3 Heat oil and brown meat in a skillet.
4 Transfer meat to a lidded casserole dish.
5 Add garlic and onion to oil and cook until onion is wilted.
6 Add rosemary and wine to skillet and cook briefly over a high heat.
7 Add tomato sauce and beef stock.
8 Stir and dissolve all brown particles.
9 Pour liquid over veal.
10 Cover tightly and bake for 2-$2\frac{1}{2}$ hours or until meat is thoroughly tender.
11 Add olives and parsley for the last 10 minutes of cooking.

Pineapple and Cucumber Mold

2 tablespoons gelatin
1 cup cold water

1 cup boiling water
¼ cup vinegar
1 teaspoon salt
juice of 1 lemon
½ teaspoon green coloring
2 cups crushed pineapple, drained
1 cup chopped cucumber
½ cup sugar

Sauce
½ teaspoon dry mustard
⅓ cup sugar
½ teaspoon salt
2 eggs, beaten
4 tablespoons lemon juice
⅓ cup cold water
dash paprika

1 Soak gelatin in cold water.
2 Add boiling water, vinegar, salt, lemon juice and coloring.
3 When gelatin thickens, add pineapple, cucumber and sugar.
4 Mix ingredients together, pour into a ring mold and chill.
5 Mix dry sauce ingredients together, then add beaten eggs, lemon juice and water.
6 Cook in a double boiler until sauce thickens.
7 Cool and add some paprika.
8 Remove mold from ring and serve with sauce.

Peas and Mushrooms

3 lb peas
boiling water
⅛ teaspoon salt
⅛ teaspoon sugar
½ lb mushrooms
2-3 tablespoons margarine

1 Cook peas, salt and sugar in as little boiling water as possible for 15-20 minutes.
2 Drain off any remaining water.
3 Sauté mushrooms in margarine. Combine peas and mushrooms, mix well and serve.

Baked Lettuce

2 tablespoons margarine
2 heads lettuce
⅛ teaspoon salt
⅛ teaspoon pepper

1 Melt margarine in a baking dish.
2 Shred lettuce and fill baking dish. Add salt and pepper.
3 Cover and bake for 1 hour.

Frosted Chocolate Cake

⅔ cup shortening
1½ cups sugar
3 eggs
2¼ cups flour
⅔ cup cocoa
¼ teaspoon baking powder
1¼ teaspoons baking soda
1 teaspoon salt
1⅓ cups water
1 teaspoon vanilla

Frosting
2 eggs
1½ cups sugar
1 tablespoon light corn syrup
⅓ cup water
1 teaspoon vanilla
½ packet chocolate bits

1 Cream shortening and sugar until fluffy.
2 Add eggs, one at a time, beating well.
3 Sift together flour, cocoa, baking powder, soda bicarbonate and salt, and mix in water and vanilla. Beat well.
4 Pour into two 8 inch layer cake pans which have been greased and floured.
5 Bake in a pre-heated oven at 350°F for 30-35 minutes. Cool.
6 To make frosting, beat eggs, sugar, corn syrup and water until mixture stands in stiff peaks.
7 Pour into a double boiler over boiling water and beat. Fold in vanilla.
8 Ice cooled cakes completely with frosting.
9 Melt chocolate bits and pour over icing.

DINNER

No.15

Serves 8

Chicken Soup
and/or
Sardine Canapés

Sweet and Sour Chicken

Pineapple and Carrot Salad

Asparagus Surprise
and/or
Red Cabbage

Apple Brown Betty

Coffee or Tea

Chicken Soup

1 large chicken, cut up
4 carrots, sliced
4 stalks celery, sliced
4 onions, sliced
3 quarts water
¼ teaspoon salt
⅛ teaspoon pepper
dash dill
parsley

1 Put chicken, cut vegetables and water into a large pot.
2 Add salt, pepper, dill and parsley.
3 Bring to the boil, and cook slowly for about 2 hours or until chicken is tender.
4 Strain and allow to cool.
5 Remove fat.
6 Remove cooked chicken and set aside for another time.
7 Serve soup hot with soda crackers.

Sardine Canapés

1 can sardines
4 hard-cooked eggs
dash red pepper
juice of 1 lemon
8 triangular slices of toast
8 anchovies

1 Pound the sardines and eggs to a paste.
2 Season with pepper and lemon juice.
3 Spread on buttered toast.
4 Top with a rolled anchovy.

Sweet and Sour Chicken

3 frying chickens, quartered
1 teaspoon chili sauce
2 teaspoons salt

¼ teaspoon pepper
½ cup melted margarine
2 large onions, sliced
1 cup water
½ cup brown sugar
1 tablespoon Worcestershire sauce
1 cup raisins
1 cup sherry
1 large can black bing cherries, pitted

1 Place chicken, skin side up, in a roasting pan.
2 Season with chili sauce, salt and pepper.
3 Pour over melted margarine.
4 Broil until brown, then turn and brown other side.
5 Combine other ingredients except cherries and sherry.
6 Pour over chicken and cover pan.
7 Bake in a pre-heated oven at 325°F for ¾ hour.
8 Marinate cherries in sherry, pour over chicken and cook uncovered for 15 minutes.

Pineapple and Carrot Salad

1 packet lemon-flavored gelatin
2 cups hot water
juice of 1 lemon
1 cup grated carrot
1 cup crushed pineapple
few grapefruit sections
mayonnaise

1 Dissolve gelatin in hot water. Add lemon juice. Set aside to cool.
2 When gelatin is cold and commencing to thicken add grated carrot and crushed pineapple.

(Continued on page 181)

Hungarian Goulash (see page 186)

3 Pour into a mold and set.
4 Unmold and serve on lettuce with a few sections of grapefruit around the outside.
5 Top with a dab of mayonnaise.

Asparagus Surprise

2 medium large fresh tomatoes
1½ lb cooked or canned asparagus
2 medium large fresh tomatoes
½ cup breadcrumbs
¼ teaspoon salt
⅛ teaspoon pepper

1 Cut tomatoes into 8 fairly thick slices across the grain.
2 Divide asparagus into 8 and place on tomato slices.
3 Sprinkle generously with breadcrumbs.
4 Season with salt and pepper.
5 Bake in a pre-heated oven at 350°F until breadcrumbs brown.
6 Serve hot.

Red Cabbage

1 head of red cabbage
4 tablespoons margarine
½ cup vinegar
½ cup brown sugar

1 Shred red cabbage.
2 Plunge into cold water for 10 minutes to crisp.
3 Drain and dry on paper toweling.
4 Melt margarine in a 4-quart saucepan.
5 Add cabbage slowly to the saucepan.

6 Cover saucepan tightly and simmer slowly for 1 hour over a moderate heat stirring often.
7 Mix vinegar and sugar and add.
8 Simmer for 30 minutes longer.

Apple Brown Betty

7 slices bread
6 cups cored, peeled, diced tart apples
¾ cup brown sugar
½ teaspoon cinnamon
¼ teaspoon salt
½ cup water
1 teaspoon almond extract
¼ cup margarine, melted

1 Remove crusts from bread and discard. Cut bread into small cubes.
2 Toast cubes lightly in a shallow pan in the oven.
3 Put third of crumbs into a buttered 9 inch round baking dish.
4 Cover crumbs with half of apples.
5 Mix sugar, cinnamon and salt together and sprinkle half of it over the apples.
6 Add another third of crumbs.
7 Spread balance of apples over crumbs.
8 Sprinkle rest of sugar mixture over apples.
9 Cover this with rest of crumbs.
10 Add almond extract to water and pour over the mixture.
11 Sprinkle melted butter over top.
12 Cover with aluminium foil.
13 Bake in a pre-heated oven at 350°F for 30 minutes.
14 Uncover and bake for an additional 15 minutes.
15 Serve warm or cold.

Lebkuchen (see page 190)

DINNER

No.16

Serves 6

Jellied Tomato Bouillon
and/or
Peas and Pasta Shells

Baked Fish in Creole Sauce

Egg Ring

Banana Fritters
and/or
Tam Gan Eden Farfel

Raisin Rice Pudding

Chocolate Coconut Kisses

Coffee or Tea

Jellied Tomato Bouillon

3 cups canned tomatoes
3 sticks celery, chopped
2 tablespoons minced carrots
2 tablespoons minced onions
sprinkle pickling spice
$\frac{1}{8}$ teaspoon salt
$\frac{1}{8}$ teaspoon pepper
$1\frac{1}{2}$ cups water
$1\frac{1}{2}$ tablespoons gelatin
$\frac{1}{4}$ cup lemon juice
paprika

1 Combine vegetables, spices and water, and cook for 15 minutes.
2 Add gelatin dissolved in lemon juice.
3 Strain through a cheesecloth and set aside to firm.
4 Serve very cold, dusted with paprika.

Peas and Pasta Shells

1 cup finely chopped onion
2 cloves garlic, crushed
$\frac{1}{4}$ cup olive oil
$\frac{1}{4}$ cup butter
8 oz pasta shells, boiled and drained
$2\frac{1}{2}$ cups peas, cooked
1 cup finely chopped parsley
$\frac{1}{2}$ teaspoon salt
$\frac{1}{4}$ teaspoon freshly ground black pepper

1 Sauté onion and garlic in combined oil and butter for 10 minutes.
2 Add pasta shells, peas, parsley, salt and pepper and mix well.
3 Pour into a casserole.
4 Cover and bake in a pre-heated oven at 350°F for 15 minutes or until hot.

Baked Fish in Creole Sauce

3 lb white fish
1 onion, chopped
1 cup celery, diced and sliced
1 green pepper, chopped
3 carrots, diced
$\frac{1}{4}$ teaspoon salt
$\frac{1}{8}$ teaspoon pepper
2 oz butter or margarine
3 cups stewed tomatoes
2 tablespoons chopped parsley

1 Place fish in a greased baking dish.
2 Add onion, celery, green pepper, carrots, salt and pepper.
3 Dot with butter.
4 Pour tomatoes over fish.
5 Bake uncovered in a pre-heated oven at 325°F for 1 hour.
6 Sprinkle with parsley.

Egg Ring

1 tablespoon plain gelatin
$\frac{1}{2}$ cup water
$\frac{1}{4}$ cup vinegar
$\frac{3}{4}$ tablespoon sugar
$\frac{1}{4}$ teaspoon dry mustard
$\frac{1}{2}$ teaspoon salt
$\frac{1}{8}$ teaspoon pepper
$\frac{1}{2}$ cup mayonnaise
8 eggs, hard-cooked

1 Soak gelatin in $\frac{1}{4}$ cup cold water.
2 Boil vinegar with $\frac{1}{4}$ cup water.
3 Add water-soaked gelatin, stir and set aside to cool.
4 Dissolve sugar and mustard and add.
5 Add salt, pepper and mayonnaise.
6 Chop eggs well and pour mixture over them; mix well.
7 Put in a ring mold and place in the refrigerator to set.
Note Egg Ring can be made the day before required.

Banana Fritters

1 cup flour, sifted
¼ cup sugar
1¼ teaspoons salt
2 teaspoons baking powder
1 egg, beaten
½ cup milk
2 tablespoons melted butter
3 bananas, cut into small pieces

1 Sift together flour, sugar, salt and baking powder.
2 Combine egg and milk and add to dry ingredients.
3 Stir until mixture is smooth.
4 Stir in butter and bananas.
5 Drop spoonfuls of mixture into deep, hot fat and fry until brown and tender.
6 Serve sprinkled with confectioners' sugar and cinnamon.

Tam Gan Eden Farfel

½ lb egg barley
boiling water
1 can condensed mushroom soup
1 can French-fried onion rings
1 tablespoon butter for casserole

1 Drop egg barley into rapidly boiling salted water.
2 Boil for 8 minutes.
3 Drain; rinse with cold water to separate.
4 Mix with undiluted mushroom soup and onion rings.
5 Reserve some onion rings for garnishing the top.

6 Place in a buttered casserole and bake in a pre-heated oven at 350°F for 20 minutes.
7 Serve.

Raisin Rice Pudding

4 cups fresh milk, OR 2 cups evaporated milk and 2 cups water
½ cup granulated sugar
½ cup uncooked rice
¼ teaspoon salt
¼ teaspoon nutmeg
2 tablespoons butter
½ cup seedless raisins
1 tablespoon butter to grease pan

1 Combine all the ingredients except the raisins and pour into a greased 1½-quart casserole.
2 Bake uncovered at 350°F for 1 hour.
3 Then add raisins and stir.
4 Bake 1½ hours longer.
5 Serve hot or cold, with or without cream.

Chocolate Coconut Kisses

1 can condensed milk
¼ lb bitter chocolate, melted
½ lb coconut
1 teaspoon vanilla

1 Combine all ingredients.
2 Drop teaspoonfuls of mixture onto a buttered cookie sheet.
3 Bake for 10 minutes in a hot oven.

DINNER

No.17

Serves 4

Cabbage Soup
and/or
Fried Calf's Brains

Hungarian Goulash

Kidney Bean Salad
and/or
Beets in Orange Sauce

Squash Pancakes

Chocolate Nut Squares

Coffee or Tea

Cabbage Soup

1½ lb head of cabbage
1½ lb flanken
1 onion, finely cut
marrow bones
⅛ teaspoon salt
dash sour salt
1 can whole peeled tomatoes
1 can tomato soup
1 can tomato sauce
½ teaspoon sugar
water

1 Shred cabbage and put in a large soup pot.
2 Add remaining ingredients.
3 Cover with water.
4 Cook for about 3 hours.
5 Skim frequently to remove scum.

Fried Calf's Brains

2 large onions
1 teaspoon chicken fat
1 set calf's brains
2 eggs
¼ teaspoon salt
⅛ teaspoon pepper

1 Cut onions finely and sauté in chicken fat.
2 Remove outer veins from brains and
   mash; add eggs and beat well.
3 Add seasonings.
4 Mix with onions.
5 Fry gently, stirring occasionally, for
   about 15 minutes.

Hungarian Goulash

2 large onions, sliced
¼ cup fat
2 lb chuck steak, cubed
1½ teaspoons salt
1 tablespoon Hungarian sweet paprika
1 x 6 oz can tomato paste

1 Sauté onions in fat until golden brown.
2 Put meat into pan and brown.
3 Add rest of ingredients.
4 Cover and simmer for 1½ hours. (If
   necessary, add ¼ cup water.)

Kidney Bean Salad

2 cups canned kidney beans
4 slices dried beef, diced
½ chopped cucumber
⅓ cup French Dressing made with basil
   wine vinegar

1 Drain beans.
2 Crisp the dried beef and chop cucumber.
3 Combine and mix with dressing.
4 Arrange on crisp lettuce and serve with
   additional French dressing. (See page 25.)

Beets in Orange Sauce

8-10 sliced beets, cooked or canned
1 small onion, grated
1 tablespoon vinegar
3 tablespoons sugar
1 tablespoon melted margarine
juice and grated rind of 1 orange
⅛ teaspoon salt

1 Mix all ingredients and place in a
   saucepan.
2 Cover tightly and simmer for 15 minutes.
3 Stir several times.

Squash Pancakes

1½ lb yellow summer squash
2 eggs, well beaten
⅛ teaspoon baking powder
2 tablespoons flour
¼ teaspoon salt
oil for frying

1 Wash and scrape squash.
2 Dice and cook slowly until tender in a small amount of salted water.
3 Drain and cool.
4 Mash and add rest of ingredients.
5 Fry thin pancakes in deep fat.

Chocolate Nut Squares

3 eggs
$\frac{1}{8}$ teaspoon salt
1 cup sugar
2 squares bitter chocolate
$\frac{1}{2}$ lb margarine
1 teaspoon vanilla
1 cup chopped nuts
1 teaspoon baking powder
$\frac{3}{4}$ cup flour

1 Beat eggs, add salt and blend in sugar.
2 Melt chocolate and add to the creamed margarine.
3 Combine both mixtures.
4 Add vanilla, nuts and flour sifted with baking powder.
5 Pour into a square or oblong shallow pan and bake in a pre-heated oven at 325°F for about 20 minutes.
6 Cut into squares while still warm.

DINNER

No. 18

Serves 6

Old-Fashioned Vegetable Soup
and/or
Baked Grapefruit

Veal Casserole

Vegetable Salad

Squash Hotcakes
and/or
String Beans with Almonds

Lebkuchen

Coffee or Tea

Old-Fashioned Vegetable Soup

2 quarts soup stock
1½ cups diced potatoes
1 cup diced celery
3 small onions
½ cup fresh peas
1½ cups canned tomatoes
½ cup shredded cabbage
¼ teaspoon salt
⅛ teaspoon pepper
2 tablespoons parsley, finely chopped

1 Heat stock.
2 Add vegetables and seasonings and cook gently until vegetables are tender.
3 Add chopped parsley and serve.

Baked Grapefruit

3 grapefruit
6 teaspoons honey
1 tablespoon cinnamon

1 Cut grapefruit in half, crosswise; cut out center core; loosen sections.
2 Spread each grapefruit half with 1 teaspoon honey and sprinkle with cinnamon.
3 Bake in a pre-heated oven at 300°F for about 10 minutes or until fruit is warm through.

Veal Casserole

1 tablespoon salad oil
3 tablespoons margarine
2 lb veal cutlets, cut in strips
3 tablespoons flour
¾ teaspoon salt
⅛ teaspoon pepper
1 cup chicken broth
1 cup dry white wine
1 small bay leaf

¼ cup minced parsley
½ lb small mushrooms
1 lb can onions

1 Heat oil and 1 tablespoon margarine in a heavy skillet and brown meat.
2 Skim pieces out with a slotted spoon and arrange in a medium casserole.
3 Blend flour and remaining margarine together in pan.
4 Stir in salt, pepper and chicken broth.
5 Stir until sauce is thick and smooth.
6 Add wine, bay leaf, parsley and mushrooms, and season to taste.
7 Pour sauce over casserole.
8 Cover and bake in a pre-heated oven at 325°F for 1 hour or until meat is tender.
9 Add onions about ½ hour before meat is cooked.

Vegetable Salad

¼ cup water
½ cup vinegar
3 tablespoons sugar
¼ teaspoon pepper
1 cup diced celery
1 cup diced carrots
3 tablespoons dressing
1 hard-cooked egg, finely chopped

1 Boil water, vinegar, sugar and pepper.
2 Pour over diced vegetables.
3 Refrigerate.
4 Serve on lettuce.
5 Add dressing and egg.

Squash Hotcakes

1 lb yellow or summer squash
½ cup pancake flour
3 eggs, separated
¼ teaspoon salt
⅛ teaspoon pepper

189

1 Wash squash. Remove browned, bruised spots.
2 Grate on a medium grater.
3 Throw away coarse seeds.
4 Add pancake flour, egg yolks and seasoning.
5 Fold in stiffly beaten egg whites.
6 Drop tablespoonfuls into frying pan.
7 Cook on both sides.
8 Serve hot.

String Beans with Almonds

1 lb string beans
½ cup sliced onion, OR 1 clove of garlic, crushed
1 teaspoon salt
½ teaspoon sugar
2 tablespoons margarine
¼ cup sliced almonds

1 Wash, string and cut the beans into 2 inch lengths.
2 Add onion or garlic and a small amount of water.
3 Season with salt and sugar, cook until tender.
4 Brown almonds in melted margarine in a skillet. Stir almonds until they are cooked and toasted.
5 Pour almonds over string beans.
6 Serve hot.

Lebkuchen

¾ cup honey
1 cup brown sugar
⅛ cup water
2 eggs, separated
3½ cups all-purpose flour
¼ teaspoon baking soda
⅛ teaspoon ground cloves

⅛ teaspoon nutmeg
½ teaspoon cinnamon
2 eggs, well beaten
4 oz shelled walnuts
4 oz candied citron, orange peel and lemon peel, finely cut
¼ cup glazed cherries

Icing
½ cup confectioners' sugar
1 tablespoon boiling water
¼ teaspoon vanilla extract

1 Boil honey, brown sugar and water for 5 minutes. Cool.
2 Add egg yolks to mixture and cream thoroughly.
3 Beat egg whites until stiff and blend into mixture.
4 Sift flour, measure and sift 3 times with soda bicarbonate.
5 Add spices, eggs, nuts, fruits (except cherries) to honey mixture. Mix well.
6 Flour hands and spread dough mixture into a shallow baking pan.
7 Bake in pre-heated oven at 350°F for about 40 minutes until cooked.
8 Cool and remove from pan.
9 Combine icing ingredients and stir until smooth. Add more water if required.
10 Ice cake.
11 Cut into pieces and garnish with glazed cherries.

DINNER

Menu

No.19

Serves 8

Consommé

Mock Seafood Extravaganza
and/or
Lamb Casserole

Tossed Green Salad

Sweet and Sour Cabbage
and/or
Individual Potato Kugels

Stewed Prunes

Mandel Brot

Coffee or Tea

Consommé

3 lb shin beef
2 tablespoons oil
6 quarts cold water
1 lb marrow bone
3 lb knuckle of veal
6 celery stalks, finely cut
1½ tablespoons salt
1 tablespoon peppercorns
6 medium onions, sliced
6 carrots, finely cut
3 bay leaves
3 sprigs parsley

1 Cut beef into small cubes and sear in oil in hot skillet until well browned.
2 Place in a large pot and add water, marrow bone, veal bone and veal meat cut in pieces.
3 Partly cover, heat slowly to boiling point.
4 Simmer gently for 5 hours, removing scum as it forms.
5 Add remaining ingredients and cook for 3 hours longer.
6 Strain through a cheesecloth and set aside to cool.
7 When nearly cool, remove the fat by drawing strips of paper toweling across the surface of the consommé, if you are in a hurry to use it. It is better to let it stand overnight, then skim off the fat.
8 The jelly may be served chilled with lemon on it, or heated to boiling and served hot.

Mock Seafood Extravaganza

2 lb fresh salmon
2 lb halibut
celery leaves
1 onion, quartered
3 stalks celery, chopped
1 hard-cooked egg, chopped
1 green pepper, chopped
1 carrot, grated

½ cup mayonnaise
lemon juice
¼ teaspoon salt

Garnish
tomato wedges
radishes
olives
Thousand Island Dressing

1 Poach fish slowly in salted water with celery leaves and onion.
2 Cool; remove bones from fish and flake flesh with a fork.
3 Add celery, egg, green pepper and carrot.
4 Thin mayonnaise with a little lemon juice, add salt and pour over.
5 Garnish with tomato wedges, radishes and olives.
6 Serve with Thousand Island Dressing. (See page 25.)

Lamb Casserole

2 lb shoulder lamb
4 tablespoons margarine
2 tablespoons brandy
1 bunch carrots
1 lb white turnips
1 lb baby onions
½ lb mushrooms
1 lb peas
½ lb green beans
1 tablespoon tomato paste
1-2 tablespoons concentrated stock
3 tablespoons flour
½ cup red wine or sherry
1 cup soup stock
½ teaspoon salt
¼ teaspoon pepper
2 tomatoes
2 tablespoons chopped chives

1 Cut meat into serving-size pieces.
2 Heat 2 tablespoons margarine in a pan; when very hot, brown meat on all sides.
3 Pour flaming brandy over meat.

4 Remove lamb and add 2 tablespoons margarine.
5 Dice carrots, turnips and onions and add.
6 Brown quickly.
7 Add quartered mushrooms, peas and beans.
8 Remove pot from stove and add tomato paste, concentrated stock and flour.
9 Pour on wine and soup stock.
10 Stir over heat until mixture comes to the boil.
11 Add lamb; season.
12 Cover and cook gently for about 1 hour or until meat is tender.
13 At the end of the cooking period, add peeled and sliced tomatoes.
14 Sprinkle with chives and serve.

Tossed Green Salad

Dressing
1 clove garlic
½ teaspoon salt
12 green olives
2 tablespoons olive oil
1 tablespoon wine vinegar
juice of ½ lime
⅛ teaspoon freshly ground pepper
dash red pepper
⅛ teaspoon thyme

Croutons
3 tablespoons olive oil
5 cloves garlic, diced
4 slices white bread, cut into cubes

1 Crush clove of garlic in a small deep bowl with salt.
2 Mince olives.
3 Add olives, oil, vinegar, lime juice and spices. Marinate dressing.
4 Heat the oil for croutons in a frying pan.
5 Brown garlic and remove it. In this oil brown the cubes of bread.
6 When well toasted set aside to cool.
7 Place salad greens in a salad bowl, pour over dressing and croutons and mix well. If desired, garnish with Italian tomatoes.

Sweet and Sour Cabbage

1 head cabbage
4 tablespoons chicken fat
2 tablespoons brown sugar
2 tablespoons flour
½ cup water
⅓ cup vinegar
¼ teaspoon salt
⅛ teaspoon pepper
1 small onion, sliced

1 Cook cabbage uncovered in boiling water for 7 minutes. Drain and set aside.
2 Heat chicken fat. Add brown sugar and flour and blend.
3 Add water, vinegar and seasonings.
4 Cook for about 5 minutes until the sauce is thick.
5 Add onion and cabbage.
6 Re-heat and serve.

Individual Potato Kugels

6 medium potatoes, boiled
4 eggs, separated
4 tablespoons chicken fat
¼ teaspoon salt
⅛ teaspoon freshly ground pepper

1 Mash potatoes until very fluffy and, while hot, add beaten egg yolks, melted fat, seasonings, and lastly, the beaten whites.
2 Grease muffin tins very well and half fill each tin with the mixture.
3 Bake in a pre-heated oven at 425°F for about 30 minutes and serve hot.

Stewed Prunes

½ lb prunes
water to cover
½ cup sugar

1 Soak prunes in water for 2 hours or overnight, if possible.
2 Ensure prunes are well covered with water.
3 Cook slowly until prunes can be pierced easily with a fork or until the seeds separate from the pulp when crushed.
4 Add sugar and continue to cook until it is completely dissolved, and then remove from the stove and cool. More sweetening may be added, if desired.

Variations
1 Cook prunes with a stick of cinnamon.
2 Add 1 teaspoon of almond extract to prunes towards end of cooking period.
3 Add 2 tablespoons of Cointreau or Amaretto during the last five minutes of cooking.
4 Cook prunes with a few lemon slices or a small amount of lemon peel.

Mandel Brot

½ cup shortening
1 cup sugar
3 eggs, beaten
juice and rind of 1 lemon
1 teaspoon vanilla extract
½ cup chopped almonds
3½ cups flour
3½ teaspoons baking powder

1 Cream shortening and sugar.
2 Add beaten eggs, lemon juice and vanilla, and nuts mixed with a little flour. Gradually add remaining dry ingredients.
3 Cut dough into 3 parts. Form into rolls.
4 Bake in a pre-heated 325°F oven for about 40 minutes.
5 Remove from pan, cut into slices 1 inch thick and return to oven until toasted a golden brown.

DINNER

No. 20

Serves 8

Stuffed Cabbage
and/or
Chicken in the Pot

Vegetable Salad

Scalloped Apples
and/or
Tante's Noodle Pudding

Coffee or Tea

Stuffed Cabbage

1 small onion, sliced
1 tablespoon margarine
1 head cabbage
$\frac{1}{2}$ lb chopped meat
1 tablespoon rice
1 egg
$\frac{1}{4}$ teaspoon salt
$\frac{1}{8}$ teaspoon pepper

Sauce
2 onions
6 dried apricots
6 prunes
$\frac{1}{4}$ cup white raisins
juice of $\frac{1}{2}$ lemon
1 can tomato sauce
1 can water
$\frac{1}{2}$ cup brown sugar
1 can tomato sauce (extra)
1 can water (extra)

1 Sauté onion in margarine.
2 Soak cabbage leaves in hot water for 5 minutes to make them less brittle.
3 Shave away thick cabbage spine on each leaf to make it easier to roll.
4 Mix all the ingredients together, except those for the sauce.
5 Roll a tablespoon of the meat mixture in each cabbage leaf.
6 To make the sauce, sauté onions in a large pot.
7 Add remaining sauce ingredients and simmer for 1 hour.
8 Add extra can tomato sauce and extra can water.
9 Dice the remaining cabbage leaves and add to the sauce. Add the rolled cabbage and cook for 2 hours. Add more lemon juice if desired.

Chicken in the Pot

2 quarts water
2 frying chickens, cut in quarters
2 lb necks, backs, giblets
2 large carrots, diced
3 celery stalks, diced
1 onion, sliced
$\frac{1}{4}$ teaspoon salt
$\frac{1}{8}$ teaspoon pepper
2 packets frozen mixed vegetables
noodles, rice or matzo balls
2 tablespoons chopped parsley

1 Boil water and add all chicken, carrots, celery, onion, salt and pepper.
2 Cover and cook until chicken is tender.
3 Remove chicken and allow necks, backs and giblets to cook for about 1 hour longer.
4 Strain off liquid and cool. Remove excess fat from pan.
5 Discard necks, backs and giblets.
6 Reheat liquid and chicken pieces. Add frozen mixed vegetables and noodles, rice or matzo balls.
7 Serve piping hot in large bowls, with one quarter of chicken and a generous quantity of vegetables for each person.
8 Garnish with chopped parsley.

Vegetable Salad

$\frac{1}{4}$ cup cold water
1 tablespoon granulated gelatin
1 cup boiling water
$\frac{1}{4}$ cup granulated sugar
$\frac{1}{2}$ teaspoon salt
3 tablespoons lemon juice
$\frac{1}{2}$ cup sliced cucumber
$\frac{1}{4}$ cup diced pimiento
1 sliced avocado
$\frac{1}{4}$ cup green pepper, diced
$\frac{1}{4}$ cup grated carrot
1 small can chop suey vegetables, drained

1 Pour cold water into bowl and sprinkle gelatin on top. Stand aside until firm.
2 Add boiling water, sugar and salt. Stir until dissolved.

(Continued on page 199)

Stuffed Cabbage (see page 104)

3 Add lemon juice and chill.

4 When slightly thickened, add vegetables.

5 Pour into a mold and chill.

6 Serve on lettuce with Thousand Island Dressing. (See page 25.)

4 Work the sugar, flour and margarine together into crumbs and spread over apples.

5 Bake in a pre-heated oven at 400°F for 30 minutes.

Scalloped Apples

4 large apples

¼ teaspoon cinnamon

¼ teaspoon salt

1 tablespoon lemon juice

¼ cup water

½ cup brown sugar

¼ cup flour

⅓ cup margarine

1 Pare, core and slice apples.

2 Place them in a greased casserole.

3 Add cinnamon, salt, lemon juice and water.

Tante's Noodle Pudding

1 lb noodles, cooked and drained

3 eggs, beaten

1 cup white raisins

3 apples, peeled, cored, and cubed

½ cup chopped almonds

½ cup cinnamon and sugar

4 tablespoons fat or margarine

2 tablespoons sugar

1 Grease casserole.

2 Pre-heat oven to 350°F.

3 Combine all ingredients and mix well.

4 Put in the casserole.

5 Bake for 1 hour in a pre-heated oven at 350°F.

6 Serve with a fruit sauce.

Baked Flounder Veronique (see page 201)

DINNER

Menu

No. 21

Serves 6

Tomato Herb Soup
and/or
Mushrooms Florentine

Baked Flounder Veronique

Herbed Rice
and/or
Cauliflower with Almonds

Sweet Potatoes in Orange Shells

Danish Pastry

Coffee or Tea

Tomato Herb Soup

3 cups tomato juice
3 cups chicken broth
2 teaspoons sugar
dash Worcestershire sauce
1 tablespoon finely chopped celery
1 tablespoon finely chopped green pepper
1 tablespoon finely chopped onion
salt and pepper to taste
1 tablespoon finely chopped parsley

1 Blend all ingredients except parsley and bring to boiling point but do not boil.
2 Sprinkle a little chopped parsley over the top and serve.

Mushrooms Florentine

1 lb fresh mushrooms
2 packets frozen spinach
1 teaspoon salt
$\frac{1}{4}$ cup chopped onion
$\frac{1}{4}$ cup melted butter
1 cup grated Cheddar cheese
$\frac{1}{8}$ teaspoon garlic salt

1 Wash and dry mushrooms.
2 Remove stems and sauté stems and caps until brown.
3 Line a shallow 10 inch casserole with spinach and seasoned with salt, onion and melted butter.
4 Sprinkle on $\frac{1}{2}$ cup grated cheese.
5 Arrange sautéed mushrooms over spinach.
6 Sprinkle with garlic salt.
7 Cover with remaining cheese.
8 Bake in a pre-heated oven for 20 minutes at 350°F.

Note: You may prepare Mushrooms Florentine in advance and refrigerate until ready to bake.

Baked Flounder Veronique

2 tablespoons onion flakes
$\frac{1}{4}$ teaspoon salt
$\frac{1}{8}$ teaspoon pepper
$2\frac{1}{2}$ lb flounder fillets
2 tablespoons butter or margarine
2 tablespoons lemon juice
$\frac{3}{4}$ cup white wine
2 tablespoons flour
1 cup light cream
green seedless grapes

1 Preheat oven to 350°F.
2 Lightly grease a baking dish and sprinkle onion flakes on the bottom of the pan.
3 Season fillets with salt and pepper and roll up.
4 Place fillets in the pan and dot with 1 tablespoon butter.
5 Combine lemon juice and wine and pour over fish.
6 Bake for about 25 minutes.
7 Melt 1 tablespoon butter or margarine in a separate skillet and add flour.
8 Add pan juices from cooked fish to flour mixture.
9 Add cream and grapes, stirring constantly until grapes are heated.
10 Pour sauce over fish and continue baking for about 5-7 minutes.

Herbed Rice

4 tablespoons margarine or butter
3 tablespoons finely chopped onions
$1\frac{1}{2}$ cups uncooked rice
$\frac{1}{2}$ tablespoon thyme
1 bay leaf
2 sprigs parsley
2 drops Tabasco sauce
3 cups chicken stock

1 Preheat oven to 400°F.
2 Melt margarine in an ovenproof saucepan or casserole and add the onion.

3 Cook, stirring, until translucent.
4 Add rice and cook for 3 minutes longer.
5 Add remaining ingredients.
6 Bring to the boil, then transfer to the oven.
7 Bake for 25 minutes or until rice is tender and fluffy.
8 Remove parsley and bay leaf and serve.

Cauliflower with Almonds

1 medium head of cauliflower
$\frac{1}{4}$ cup salted almonds
1 cup medium white sauce
paprika or grated cheese

1 Trim leaves from cauliflower, leaving 1 inch of stem for support.
2 In a large saucepan add hot water to cover stem but not touching head.
3 Cover closely and steam for about 25 minutes or until tender.
4 Cut off stem and place flowerets in a serving dish.
5 Stick almonds in the cauliflower or cut into thin slivers and sprinkle over the top.
6 Pour over white sauce, sprinkle with paprika or cheese, and serve.

Sweet Potatoes in Orange Shells

6 medium sweet potatoes
1 cup crushed pineapple
salt and pepper to taste
2 tablespoons margarine
8 orange shells
marshmallows

1 Mix mashed sweet potatoes with crushed pineapple. Add margarine and season to taste with salt and pepper.

2 Prepare halves of orange shells by removing fruit pulp. Cut shells into fancy points by using a small knife.
3 Fill with sweet potato mixture, top with 2 marshmallows and heat in the oven until very hot and the marshmallows are toasted and brown.

Danish Pastry

1 packet yeast
$\frac{1}{2}$ cup warm milk
$\frac{1}{2}$ lb butter
1 tablespoon sugar
2 cups flour, sifted
1 teaspoon salt
3 eggs, separated
1 cup sugar
$\frac{1}{2}$ cup chopped walnuts
$\frac{1}{2}$ cup chopped raisins

1 Dissolve yeast in warm milk.
2 Cream butter and sugar, add flour and salt.
3 Add milk mixture and egg yolks. Blend.
4 Put into the refrigerator overnight.
5 When ready to bake, divide dough into 3 parts.
6 Roll out each part into a flat leaf. Spread with a mixture of egg whites and sugar, and sprinkle with walnuts and raisins or jelly.
7 Roll and cut.
8 Bake for about 40 minutes in a pre-heated oven at 350°F.

DINNER

Menu

No. 22

Serves 6

Mushroom Soup
and/or
Fried Herring

Barbequed Ribs of Beef

Greens and Grapes Salad

Potato Kugels
and/or
Fried Apples

Cranberry Tea Meringues

Coffee or Tea

Mushroom Soup

2 lb soup meat, beef bones and marrow
bones
3 quarts boiling water
1 cup dried lima beans
1 oz dried mushrooms
1 tablespoon salt
3 carrots, diced
½ lb fresh peas
1 parsnip, diced
1 piece celery root, diced
½ cup celery, diced
½ can tomatoes, strained
1 onion, finely cut
2 tablespoons fine barley

1 Cover meat and bones with boiling water
and cook until meat is tender.
2 Remove meat and bones. Add lima beans.
3 Scald mushrooms and cut into small
pieces. Add to soup.
4 Cook for 2-2½ hours over a low heat.
5 Add salt, vegetables and washed barley.
6 Cook for 1 hour longer.
Note: Reserve meat for other uses such as
stuffed cabbage.

Fried Herring

2 salt herrings
2 small onions, thinly sliced
2 tablespoons butter
1 hard-cooked egg, minced
¼ cup light cream

1 Cover herring in water and soak for 24
hours. Change water twice during this
time.
2 Drain.
3 Dry herring and carefully remove bones,
heads and tails. Cut herring into portions
for serving.
4 Sauté onions in butter in a skillet until
tender but very lightly browned.
5 Add herring; cook for 5 minutes, turning
once.

6 Add egg and cream.
7 Cook for 5 minutes longer.
8 Serve at once.

Barbequed Ribs of Beef

3 lb short ribs
2 teaspoons salt
2 tablespoons fat
¼ teaspoon pepper
1 teaspoon paprika
1 teaspoon dry mustard
1 tablespoon sugar
1 tablespoon Worcestershire sauce
½ cup catsup
½ cup water
¼ cup cider vinegar
½ cup minced onions
1 clove garlic, minced

1 Brown the ribs in fat in a heated casserole
or Dutch oven.
2 Pour off the fat.
3 Combine all the remaining ingredients.
4 Add them to the ribs.
5 Cover and bake in a pre-heated oven at
350°F for 2 hours.
6 Remove the cover for the last half hour of
cooking.

Greens and Grapes Salad

1 head Romaine lettuce
1 x 10 oz packet fresh spinach
1 lb green seedless grapes

Dressing
⅔ cup vegetable oil
⅓ cup cider vinegar
1 teaspoon salt
1 teaspoon sugar
1 teaspoon dry mustard
½ teaspoon basil
¼ teaspoon paprika

1 Combine ingredients for dressing the day
before serving and refrigerate.

2 Wash lettuce and spinach thoroughly to get rid of sand.
3 Cut the stems off the spinach leaves.
4 Dry on paper towelling.
5 Break lettuce and spinach into bite-size pieces and add grapes.
6 Toss with dressing before serving.

Potato Kugels

6 medium potatoes, boiled
4 eggs, separated
4 tablespoons chicken fat
$\frac{1}{4}$ teaspoon salt
$\frac{1}{8}$ teaspoon freshly ground pepper

1 Mash potatoes until they are very fluffy and, while hot, add beaten egg yolks, melted fat, seasonings and, lastly, the beaten whites.
2 Grease individual muffin tins very well and half fill each tin with the mixture.
3 Bake in a pre-heated oven at 325°F for about 30 minutes.
4 Serve hot.

Fried Apples

2 cans sliced apples, including juice
1 cup sugar
juice and rind of $\frac{1}{2}$ lemon
2 tablespoons margarine
$\frac{1}{8}$ teaspoon salt

1 Combine ingredients in a skillet.
2 Cook at 350°F or a medium heat until apples brown on the bottom.
3 Serve.

Cranberry Tea Meringues

2 cups sifted enriched flour
$\frac{1}{2}$ cup sugar
$\frac{1}{4}$ teaspoon salt
$\frac{1}{2}$ teaspoon baking powder
1 cup shortening
1 cup jellied cranberry sauce
2 egg whites
$\frac{1}{4}$ cup sugar
$\frac{1}{2}$ cup chopped nuts
$\frac{1}{2}$ cup slightly crushed corn flakes

1 Combine and sift flour, $\frac{1}{2}$ cup sugar, salt, and baking powder.
2 Cut shortening in with two knives or a pastry blender. Combine thoroughly as no liquid is used.
3 Press into a lightly greased shallow pan 11 inch x 8$\frac{1}{2}$ inch x 1$\frac{1}{4}$ inch. Bake in a pre-heated oven at 350°F.
4 Spread lightly with crushed cranberry sauce.
5 Top with a nut-cereal meringue made by beating egg whites until stiff, and adding $\frac{1}{4}$ cup sugar gradually.
6 Fold in nuts and cereal.
7 Bake in a pre-heated oven at 350°F for 15-20 minutes until meringue is slightly browned.
8 When cool cut in squares.

DINNER

No. 23

Serves 6

Jellied Soup
and/or
Deviled Eggs

Sweet and Sour Salmon

Mint Slaw

Finnish Turnip Casserole
and/or
Eggplant Relish

Cheeseless Cheese Cake

Coffee or Tea

Jellied Soup

1 beef shank bone
1 veal shank bone
6 stalks celery tops
1 bunch small carrots, cleaned and pared
2 cups water
$\frac{3}{4}$ teaspoon mixed pickling spices
1 teaspoon Kitchen Bouquet
2 tomatoes
$\frac{1}{8}$ teaspoon salt
$\frac{1}{8}$ teaspoon pepper
2 tablespoons chopped parsley

1 In a soup pot combine all the ingredients except parsley.
2 Cover tightly and cook over a low heat for 4-5 hours.
3 Skim off scum as cooking progresses.
4 After cooking, uncover and stand for 2-3 hours.
5 Skim again.
6 Strain through a fine sieve or cheese cloth.
7 Cool and refrigerate.
8 Serve garnished with chopped parsley.

Deviled Eggs

3 hard-cooked eggs
1 tablespoon chopped parsley
3 tablespoons softened butter or margarine
$\frac{1}{2}$ clove garlic, finely chopped
2 finely chopped anchovies
1 tablespoon capers
mayonnaise to taste
12 strips of pimiento, about 2 inch x $\frac{1}{4}$ inch

1 Slice eggs in half lengthwise and remove yolks.
2 Blend yolks with remaining ingredients to form a smooth paste.
3 Stuff yolk mixture into egg white halves.
4 Serve stuffed egg halves on lettuce leaves.
5 Garnish with 2 pimiento strips over each egg.

Sweet and Sour Salmon

2 stalks celery with leaves
1 medium onion, sliced
2 carrots, cut in $\frac{1}{4}$ inch slices
3 sprigs parsley
2 tablespoons vinegar
3 lb salmon, sliced
$\frac{1}{2}$ cup brown sugar
6 ginger snaps
$\frac{1}{2}$ cup seedless raisins
juice of 1 lemon

Garnish
toasted almond slivers
lemon wedges
carrot rounds

1 Cook celery, onion, carrots and parsley in salted water for 15 minutes.
2 Add vinegar and salmon slices.
3 Add water to cover fish and poach gently over a low heat for about 12 minutes or until fish is cooked.
4 If fish becomes soft add a tablespoon of vinegar to liquid.
5 Remove fish carefully and reserve liquid.
6 In another saucepan put brown sugar, ginger snaps, raisins, lemon juice and enough hot liquid to dissolve ingredients.
7 Stir and cook over a low heat.
8 Add more sugar or vinegar if a stronger sweet-sour flavor is desired.
9 Pour this mixture over fish.
10 Garnish with toasted almond slivers, lemon wedges and carrot rounds.

Mint Slaw

1 medium head white cabbage
2 sprigs mint

Dressing
1 cup thick sour cream
2 tablespoons vinegar
$\frac{1}{2}$ teaspoon salt
1 tablespoon sugar

1 Shred cabbage into thin, fine strips with a sharp knife or a shredder.
2 Wash mint and chop finely.
3 Mix cabbage and mint thoroughly.
4 Mix dressing ingredients thoroughly and pour over the minted cabbage.
5 Toss lightly until well mixed and serve.

Finnish Turnip Casserole

2½-3 lb yellow turnip
2 eggs, well beaten
2 tablespoons cream
2 teaspoons nutmeg
¼ teaspoon salt
2 tablespoons butter or margarine

1 Peel turnip, cut up, and boil in lightly salted water until just soft enough to mash.
2 Beat in eggs, cream, nutmeg and salt until the mixture is light and fluffy.
3 Pour turnip mixture into a well-buttered dish, dot with butter, and bake in a pre-heated oven at 350°F for about 45 minutes or until well set.

Eggplant Relish

1 medium eggplant
1 small onion
2 center stalks celery
½ green pepper
1 tablespoon olive oil
3 tablespoons vinegar
1 teaspoon salt
1 tablespoon sugar
⅛ teaspoon pepper

1 Bake eggplant in a pre-heated oven at 400°F until soft.
2 Turn frequently to prevent burning.
3 Place in a bowl and peel when cool enough to touch.

4 Combine eggplant and other ingredients in a chopping bowl and chop until fine or put through a food grinder with a medium blade.

Cheeseless Cheese Cake

18 Graham crackers, finely crushed
¼ lb melted butter
¼ cup sugar
1 x 14 oz can sweet condensed milk
juice of 2 lemons
1 teaspoon vanilla
4 eggs, separated

1 Mix crackers with butter and sugar.
2 Line bottom and sides of a springform cake pan with ¾ of the cracker crumbs.
3 Mix together condensed milk, lemon juice, vanilla and egg yolks.
4 Beat egg whites until stiff and fold into mixture.
5 Pour batter into cake pan and sprinkle remaining crumbs on top.
6 Put into a pre-heated oven and bake at 350°F for 35 minutes.

DINNER

No. 24

Serves 6

Russian Borscht
and/or
Lemon Baskets

Braised Shoulder of Lamb

Cranberry Salad

Carrot Pudding
and/or
Tomato, Eggplant and Zucchini Salad

Topsy-Turvy Nut and Fruit Cake

Coffee or Tea

Russian Borscht

1 quart consommé
2 large beets, chopped
1 cup chopped cabbage
2 onions, chopped
1 tablespoon finely chopped parsley

1 Cook the vegetables until tender in the consommé, adding water if necessary.
2 Strain if desired.
3 Serve in traditional pottery bowls.
4 Garnish with finely chopped parsley.

Lemon Baskets

6 lemons
2 cans skinless, boneless sardines
2 tablespoons mayonnaise
6 sprigs watercress, finely chopped
1 tablespoon lemon juice

1 Cut two pieces from each lemon to make a basket shape with a handle.
2 Scoop out pulp, being careful not to break the basket form.
3 Submerge baskets in cold water until ready to fill.
4 Mash sardines moistened with mayonnaise into a fine paste.
5 Add finely chopped watercress and lemon juice.
6 Stuff the lemon baskets with the mixture.
7 Serve on a lettuce leaf.

Braised Shoulder of Lamb

1 x 2-3 lb shoulder of lamb
2 garlic cloves, slivered
$\frac{1}{2}$ cup olive oil
$\frac{1}{2}$ cup soy sauce
$\frac{1}{2}$ cup dry sherry
2 tablespoons ground ginger
2 onions studded with cloves
1 parsley sprig

1 Preheat oven to 300°F.
2 Wipe lamb with damp cloth and make incisions in several places.
3 Insert garlic slivers and rub with 2 tablespoons of oil.
4 Mix soy sauce, sherry and ginger in a bowl.
5 Marinate meat for 4 hours, turning occasionally.
6 Remove lamb from marinade and wipe with paper towels.
7 Reserve marinade.
8 Brown lamb in remaining oil.
9 Add onions, parsley and reserved marinade.
10 Cover pan and simmer meat in a preheated oven at 325°F for 2 hours.
11 Remove lamb to a hot platter and pour juices over it before serving.

Cranberry Salad

1 lb cranberries
2 tablespoons gelatin
$\frac{1}{4}$ cup cold water or pineapple juice
1 can grated pineapple
1 cup chopped celery
1 cup chopped apples
1 cup chopped walnuts

1 Cook cranberries to a pulp and purée.
2 Soak gelatin in cold water or pineapple juice for 5 minutes.
3 Dissolve gelatin mixture in cranberry purée.
4 Mix thoroughly.
5 Add other ingredients.
6 Pour into a mold and chill.
7 Unmold onto a platter surrounded by crisp lettuce leaves.

Carrot Pudding

$1\frac{1}{2}$ cups shortening
$\frac{3}{4}$ cup brown sugar
2 cups flour

1½ teaspoons baking powder
¾ teaspoon baking soda
1½ teaspoons salt
2 cups grated raw carrot
2 eggs
juice and rind of 1½ lemons

1 Cream shortening.
2 Add brown sugar
3 Sift together flour, baking powder, soda
   bicarbonate and salt, and add.
4 Mix carrots, eggs, lemon juice and rind.
5 Blend with flour mixture.
6 Pour into a well-greased mold or springform pan.
7 Bake in a pre-heated oven at 350°F for 45
   minutes-1 hour.

Tomato, Eggplant and Zucchini Salad

⅓ cup olive oil
2 cloves garlic, minced
1 eggplant, skinned and diced
½ lb zucchini, diced
2 Bermuda onions, sliced
1 green pepper, seeded and diced
1½ lb tomatoes, skinned and diced
1 tablespoon chopped fresh basil, OR 1
   teaspoon dried basil
1 tablespoon chopped fresh tarragon, OR
   1 teaspoon dried tarragon
1 tablespoon sugar
⅛ teaspoon freshly ground pepper
¼ teaspoon salt

1 Preheat oven to 375°F.
2 Place olive in a large skillet and sauté
   garlic, eggplant, zucchini, onions and
   green pepper until barely tender.
3 Place half the tomatoes in the bottom of a
   greased baking dish.
4 Sprinkle with half the basil, tarragon,
   salt and pepper.
5 Top with sautéed vegetables and then the
   remaining tomato slices and seasonings.
6 Bake for 15 minutes.

7 Reduce heat to 350°F and bake until
   tomatoes are cooked and vegetables are
   hot and bubbly.

Topsy-Turvy Nut and Fruit Cake

¼ lb margarine
1 cup brown sugar
1 cup chopped pecan nuts or walnuts
1 can shredded pineapple, sliced peaches
   or apricots
4 eggs, separated
1 cup sugar
1 cup pastry or cake flour
1 teaspoon baking powder
2 tablespoons fruit juice
½ teaspoon lemon extract

1 Melt margarine in a saucepan and add
   brown sugar.
2 Bring margarine and sugar to the boil, but
   do not overcook or mixture will have a
   bitter taste.
3 Remove from the heat. Add nuts.
4 Drain fruit and reserve juice. Add fruit to
   mixture.
5 Blend well and spread the mixture evenly
   over the bottom of a 10 inch cake pan.
6 Beat egg yolks until they are light and
   lemon-colored. Gradually add sugar.
7 Combine flour and baking powder and
   add.
8 Heat fruit juice. Add it to the mixture
   and continue to beat until all the
   ingredients have been thoroughly mixed.
9 Beat egg whites until light and stiff and
   fold into mixture.
10 Add lemon extract.
11 Pour this mixture into the cake pan over
    the other mixture. Put the pan into a pre-
    heated oven and bake for about 35
    minutes at 350°F.
12 When cooked stand cake aside for 10
    minutes. Turn cake out upside down onto
    a cake plate. The fruit will be on top.
13 Garnish with a fruit and nut border.

DINNER

No. 25

Serves 8

Baked Potato Soup
and/or
Stuffed Avocado

Fillet of Sole in Champagne Sauce

Celery Root Salad

Wild Rice with Mushrooms
and/or
String Bean Casserole

Rugalach

Coffee or Tea

Baked Potato Soup

1 large baked potato
2 cups vegetable stock
1 egg yolk
½ cup cream
1 tablespoon chopped parsley
1 teaspoon sugar
¼ teaspoon salt
⅛ teaspoon pepper

1 Mash a soft, mealy freshly baked potato in a sieve.
2 Add vegetable stock.
3 Beat egg yolk, cream and parsley and add to stock.
4 Bring to the boil. Add seasonings and serve.

Stuffed Avocado

5 tablespoons Roquefort cheese, crumbled
3 tablespoons cream cheese
5 tablespoons butter or margarine
dash Tabasco sauce
1 teaspoon white horseradish
⅛ teaspoon salt
4 medium avocados

1 Blend Roquefort cheese, cream cheese and butter in an electric blender or with a fork.
2 Add tabasco, horseradish and salt.
3 Mix well.
4 Peel and halve the avocados. Remove the stone.
6 Fill the center holes with cheese mixture.
7 Serve on crisp lettuce leaves.

Fillet of Sole in Champagne Sauce

8 fillets of sole
3 shallots or 1 onion, minced
½ lb mushrooms, sliced

1 teaspoon salt
¼ teaspoon white pepper
½ bottle champagne
juice of ½ lemon
4 oz butter
3 tablespoons flour
2 egg yolks
½ cup cream

Garnish
lemon wedges

1 Preheat oven to 400°F.
2 Cut fillets in half lengthwise and roll up. Fasten with toothpicks.
3 Butter a large oven dish and sprinkle with shallots and mushrooms.
4 Place rolled fish in dish.
5 Sprinkle fish with salt and pepper.
6 Pour on champagne and lemon juice.
7 Cover and bake for 20 minutes.
8 Remove to a heated serving dish.
9 Melt butter.
10 Add flour and cook gently for 2 minutes.
11 Add pan juices and cook, stirring until thickened.
12 Beat egg yolks into cream.
13 Add to sauce and cook, stirring over a low flame until thickened.
14 Season to taste and pour over fish. Garnish with lemon wedges.

Celery Root Salad

1 cup mayonnaise
½ cup evaporated milk
⅛ teaspoon salt
⅛ teaspoon pepper
1 cup diced cooked celery root
½ cup raw apple
1 cup diced grapefruit
1 cup diced orange
½ cup chopped walnuts
½ cup grated American cheese

1 Combine mayonnaise, evaporated milk, salt and pepper.
2 Mix celery root, apple, grapefruit, orange and walnuts.

3 Pour dressing over salad and toss lightly.
4 Sprinkle cheese thickly over the top and serve.

Wild Rice with Mushrooms

1 cup wild rice
6 cups boiling water
2 teaspoons salt
12 mushrooms, sliced
1 tablespoon butter
½ cup cream
⅛ teaspoon pepper

1 Cook rice in rapidly boiling salted water for 20 minutes, stirring occasionally to prevent scorching or lumping. Skim frequently.
2 Simmer mushrooms in butter for 5 minutes.
3 Drain rice and add it to mushrooms and the mushroom liquid.
4 Add cream and pepper.
5 Allow mixture to stand in a double boiler over hot water for at least 5 minutes before it is served.

String Bean Casserole

2 packets frozen French-style string beans
1 can cream of mushroom soup
½ can water
1 can water chestnuts, drained
1 can French-fried onion rings

1 Cook string beans in salted water according to instructions on the packet and drain.

2 Add mushroom soup diluted with ½ can water.
3 Slice chestnuts and add to beans.
4 Mix thoroughly.
5 Put in a buttered casserole and bake in a pre-heated oven at 350°F for 30 minutes.
6 Remove from the oven, put onion rings on top and return to the oven for 10 minutes.

Rugalach

¼ lb butter
¼ lb cream cheese
1 cup regular flour, sifted
¼ teaspoon salt
3 tablespoons sugar
½ cup raisins
½ cup chopped pecan nuts or walnuts

1 Cream the butter and cheese.
2 Add flour, salt and sugar and work the mixture with your hands.
3 Divide the dough and roll out onto a lightly floured board.
4 Fold each part, put in wax paper and refrigerate overnight.
5 Pre-heat oven to 375°F.
6 Roll out dough, one piece at a time, to ⅛ inch thickness.
7 Cut into triangles.
8 Fill triangle with tablespoon of raisins and chopped nuts.
9 Pinch the corners together.
10 Bake on an ungreased cookie sheet for 20 minutes.

Note: Prune mixture or other preserves can be used as filling.

Cranberry Tea Meringues (see page 205)

214

DINNER

No. 26

Serves 6

Beef and Barley Soup

Pickled Fish
and/or
Curried Beef Stew

Caviar and Egg Salad

Beets and Greens
and/or
Corn Fritters Supreme

Gelatin Fruit Mold

Spritz Cookies

Coffee or Tea

Carrot Pudding (see page 210-1)

Beef and Barley Soup

    3 short ribs or flanken
    3 quarts water
    1 teaspoon salt
    1 medium onion
    1 cup barley
    1 can corn
    1 large can whole tomatoes
    ¼ cup sugar
    2 stalks celery
    2 large carrots
    ½ can string beans
    ½ can peas
    ½ can tomato soup

 1 Put ribs in water with salt.
 2 Boil and skim.
 3 Add onion and barley.
 4 Cook for 30 minutes.
 5 Add corn, tomatoes and sugar.
 6 Cook for 1 hour.
 7 Add celery and carrots.
 8 Cook for 30 minutes.
 9 Add beans, peas and tomato soup.
10 Cook for 30 minutes.
11 Ladle into soup bowls and serve.

Pickled Fish

    1 cup white vinegar
    1 cup water
    ½ teaspoon salt
    10 peppercorns
    9 allspice berries
    2 bay leaves
    3 slices onion
    2 slices lemon
    2 lb fish, sliced
    onion slices

 1 Combine vinegar, water, salt, peppercorns, allspice berries, bay leaves and onion. Bring to the boil and simmer for 30 minutes.
 2 Add lemon, cook for 5 minutes and remove.

 3 Simmer fish in this liquid until tender. Cook only a few slices of fish at a time.
 4 Pack cooked fish into a large glass jar or stone crock with 1 or more slices of onion between layers.
 5 Pour the hot liquid with seasonings over the fish.
 6 Cover and store in a cool place. In a few days the liquid will form a jelly around the fish.

Note: Pickerel, weakfish or salmon may be used.

Curried Beef Stew

    2 tablespoons flour
    2¼ teaspoons salt
    1 teaspoon pepper
    3 lb stew beef, cut into 1 inch cubes
    1 cup oil
    4 cups sliced onion
    1 garlic clove, minced
    2 teaspoons curry powder
    2 beef bouillon cubes
    2 cups boiling water
    1 cup tomato juice

    Boiled rice
    2 quarts water
    1 teaspoon salt
    1 tablespoon lemon juice
    1 cup white rice

 1 Combine flour, salt and pepper.
 2 Dredge meat in mixture.
 3 Brown meat in oil in a 10 inch skillet.
 4 Transfer meat to a large, heavy saucepan.
 5 Add onion and garlic and sauté.
 6 Sprinkle curry powder over meat.
 7 Add bouillon cubes and water and simmer for about 1½ hours.
 8 Add tomato juice and reheat.
 9 To cook the rice, bring water, salt and lemon juice to the boil.
10 Slowly add rice, stir once or twice, reduce heat to low and half cover saucepan.
11 Cook for 20 minutes.

12 Pour cooked rice into a colander and rinse.
13 Put rice in a baking dish and heat in the oven for 20 minutes.
14 Serve Curried Stew over rice with chopped onion, relish, raisins, olives, pineapple chunks and coconut.

Caviar and Egg Salad

12 egg whites
6 tablespoons caviar
1 teaspoon grated onion
1 teaspoon lemon juice
6 lettuce leaves
3 egg yolks, hard-cooked

1 Fill well-buttered individual ring molds with unbeaten egg whites, allowing 2 whites for each mold.
2 Bake in a moderate oven for about 10 minutes or until firm.
3 Cool and remove from molds onto crisp lettuce leaves.
4 Fill centers with caviar which has been mixed with grated onion and lemon juice.
5 Cook the egg yolks in salted water, just below boiling point.
6 When hard, rub through a sieve.
7 Sprinkle over the caviar and serve very cold.

Beets and Greens

2 bunches young, tender beets with greens
1 quart water
2 tablespoons wine vinegar
½ cup dry breadcrumbs

1 Wash beets and greens under cold water.
2 Boil beets and their greens in water until beets are tender when tested with a fork.
3 Chop beets and greens.
4 Season with wine vinegar.
5 Serve topped with a sprinkling of bread-crumbs.

Corn Fritters Supreme

1 egg
2 tablespoons sugar
½ teaspoon salt
1 cup creamed corn
1 cup flour
3 teaspoons baking powder
½ cup peanut oil

1 Mix egg, sugar, salt and corn.
2 Add flour sifted with the baking powder.
3 Drop spoonfuls of mixture into hot peanut oil and cook until fritters are light golden brown.
4 Drain and serve.

Gelatin Fruit Mold

2 packets strawberry-flavored gelatin
fresh strawberries or other fruit
1 quart melon balls

1 Make gelatin according to directions on the packet.
2 Wash and hull strawberries.
3 Pour gelatin into individual molds. Fill ⅔ full.
4 Add fruit.
5 Refrigerate for 2-4 hours until set.
6 To unmold, dip mold in warm water almost to the edge.
7 Cover mold with a plate and turn upside down to release mold.

Spritz Cookies

2¼ cups sifted enriched flour
½ teaspoon baking powder
¼ teaspoon salt
1 cup margarine
¾ cup sugar
1 egg
1 teaspoon almond or vanilla extract

219

1 Combine and sift flour, baking powder and salt.
2 Cream margarine.
3 Add sugar gradually, cream thoroughly.
4 Blend in egg and extract.
5 Add sifted dry ingredients.
6 Mix well.
7 Chill dough for 1 hour.
8 Force dough through a cookie press onto an ungreased baking sheet.
9 Bake in a pre-heated oven at 400°F for 10-12 minutes.

COOKING TERMS

Almondine
With almonds or a sauce incorporating almonds.

Au Gratin
With a browned covering or crust of bread-crumbs mixed with margarine or butter or cheese. Frequently applied to a scalloped dish.

Bagel
A special bread, round in shape, with a hole like a doughnut, that is first boiled in water and then baked in the oven.

Bake
To cook by dry heat, usually in an oven; when applied to meats it is called roasting.

Barbecue
To roast meat slowly on a spit or over coals, usually basting it with a highly seasoned sauce.

Baste
To brush or ladle liquid over food while it is cooking to keep it from drying out; usually the liquid is melted fat, and meat drippings, water, water and fat or a special sauce may be used.

Beat
To mix vigorously using a rapid rotary motion or a circular, lifting motion which incorporates air; to use a food mixer or an egg beater.

Blanch
To plunge into boiling water for a few minutes, drain and then rinse in cold water. Frequently used to loosen skins of nuts and fruits; also sets color.

Blend
To combine two or more ingredients thoroughly.

Blintzes
Thin, crepe-like pancakes filled with cheese, potatoes or preserved and fried to a golden brown.

Boil
To cook in liquid above boiling point; a rapid boil signifies a continuous rapid boil.

Borscht
A soup made with beets and having a meat base. It can also be a soup with a beet base that is served with a dollop of sour cream.

Bouillon
A clear meat broth delicately seasoned.

Braise
To brown meat in a small amount of fat to which a small amount of water is added. It is simmered closely covered, at a low temperature until tender.

Bread
To roll in bread, crackers or matzo crumbs before cooking or frying.

Brine
A solution of salt and water used for preserving meats and vegetables.

Brochette
A small spit or skewer used for roasting or broiling meats.

Broil
To cook directly under a flame or over high heat or between two heat surfaces.

Broth
A thin soup; also the thin liquid in which meat, fish and vegetables are cooked.

Brown
To sauté, fry, toast, broil or bake food so that it acquires a brown color.

Brush
To spread thinly.

Canapé
An appetizer made by covering small pieces of bread, plain or toasted, with well-seasoned spreads and fancy garnishes.

Caramelize
To melt sugar slowly over a low heat until it becomes golden brown.

Casserole
A dish for baking that can be either glass, earthenware or metal; a combination of foods, frequently baked with a cream sauce.

Challah
A white loaf of bread, usually prepared for the Sabbath, that is made in a variety of shapes—twist, round, braided and plain.

Chop
To cut into fine pieces with a knife or a special cutter.

Chutney
A combination of fruit and vegetables, usually highly seasoned and of an oriental origin; a sweet pickle relish.

Citron
A sub-tropical fruit that has been candied; frequently used in fruit cakes, cookies, candies and puddings.

Coat
To dip food into seasoned flour until all sides are covered evenly: to dip foods into milk or lightly beaten egg, then in seasoned crumbs.

Compote
A dessert of fruits (usually dried fruits) cooked in a heavy syrup; also a serving dish used for preserves, candies and fruits.

Confectioners' sugar
A very fine, highly pulverized sugar that is combined with corn starch and primarily used to ice cakes; can be identified by markings on the box, ranging from XXXX to XXXXXX —the more X's the finer the texture.

Conserve
Very much like a compote, with the addition of raisins and nuts.

Consommé
A clear broth made from two or more meats and highly seasoned.

Court bouillon
A seasoned broth made from fish, and one in which fish is cooked.

Cream
The blending of butter or margarine with sugar, generally used in baking.

Croutons
Bread cut into small cubes and toasted, generally used as a garnish for soups.

Crumb
To coat a food with crumbs, such as a casserole dish before baking.

Cut and fold
The procedure of cutting down to the bottom of the bowl with a spoon or other implement and bringing the mixture up the side of the bowl so that it ends up on top. This motion is repeated to blend a mixture without loss of air, as when blending stiffly beaten egg whites into a cake batter.

Cut in shortening
To mix margarine or butter into a flour mixture with a knife or a pastry blender.

Devil
A method of making food hot or highly seasoned, such as a deviled egg.

Dice
To cut into small, uniform cubed pieces.

Drain
To free from liquid.

Dredge
To coat with flour or fine breadcrumbs, or to sprinkle or roll food in sugar or a cinnamon-sugar combination.

Einbren
Cooking flour with fat, butter or margarine, until it becomes light brown.

Escallop
Food in a casserole with sauce that is topped with fine breadcrumbs; also tomatoes that have been peeled and topped with crumbs.

Essig fleisch
Sweet and sour meat, usually potted.

Farfel
Noodle dough cut into $\frac{1}{4}$ inch square pieces.

Fillet
A boneless piece of meat or fish.

Flake
When referring to fish it means that the cooked fish should separate readily when touched with a fork.

Fleischigs
Meat or meat derivatives; also dishes made with meat products.

Florentine
Foods made with spinach.

Flute
Pressing the edge of pastry dough between thumb and forefinger to make a decorative edging.

Fold
See cut and fold.

Forshpeis
An appetizer.

French fry
To fry in deep fat.

Fricassee
To braise meat or poultry, which has been cut into small pieces, and to simmer it in its own gravy.

Fritter
A fruit or vegetable which is rolled in breadcrumbs and fried in deep fat.

Frost
Either a sugar syrup or a blend of sugar and butter or margarine used to decorate a cake.

Fry
To cook food in fat, using more fat than is used in sautéing and less fat than is used in deep frying.

Garnish
To decorate food or embellish a platter of food.

Gebrattens
Roasted meat.

Gedempte fleisch
Stewed meat.

Gefilte fish
Chopped fish, usually of several varieties, made into balls or patties.

Gehakte
Chopped, usually when referring to liver.

Glaze
Gelatinous substance from meat that accumulates in a frying or roasting pan during cooking; also refers to icing used on cakes and cookies.

Goulash
A highly seasoned stew made from cubes of meat and diced vegetables.

Grate
To reduce food to fine particles by rubbing it over the surface of a grater; generally applies to vegetables and rinds of oranges and lemons.

Gravy
A sauce made from cooking meat, poultry or fish and thickened with flour or cornstarch.

Grieben
Cracklings from rendered chicken or goose fat.

Grill
To broil or pan fry.

Halke
Dumplings made of grated potato or matzo meal. (Also known as knaidlach or knoedel.)

Hamantaschen
Triangular cakes, shaped like a three-cornered hat and filled with poppy seeds and honey or prune preserves. Usually prepared and served during Purim.

Hekhsherim
Certificate of Kashruth.

Ingberlach
Candy made with ginger and carrots.

Kasha
Cooked buckwheat groats used as a garnish with meat or as a cereal.

Kishke
Stuffed large beef intestine, usually filled with flour and fat, seasoned with onions, salt and pepper, and roasted in the oven.

Knaidlach or knoedel
Dumplings, see halke.

Knead
To work and fold over dough until it is smooth and prepared for baking of bread and rolls.

Knish
A patty that has been stuffed with potatoes or kasha and baked; also thinly rolled, stretch dough filled with chopped, seasoned meat and served in or with soup.

Kosher
Foods that have been selected and prepared in accordance with the dietary laws.

Kreplach
Noodle dough cut in small squares, stuffed with chopped meat, vegetable or cheese filling and cooked in soups or fried.

Kuchen
Cake, generally refers to coffee cake.

Kugel
A baked pudding usually made of noodles or potatoes and baked.

Latkes
Pancakes made of grated potato or matzo meal and fried.

Leavening agent
Baking powder, baking soda or yeast with sugar. Used in baking to make products light and porous.

Lekach
Honey cake.

Mandlen
Soup nuts.

Marinade
Usually a mixture of vinegar or lemon juice and water, or a well-seasoned oil and vinegar dressing in which certain foods are seasoned. Fruits may be soaked in a sweetened marinade of juices, wines and spirits.

Marinate
Soaking foods in a seasoned liquid (marinade).

Mash
To beat to a purée or to press out the lumps in foods such as potatoes or carrots.

Mask
To cover completely, usually with mayonnaise or a thick sauce.

Matzo
Flat bread made of unleavened flour.

Melt
A process of reducing solid foodstuffs by the application of heat to liquefy.

Meringue
A stiffly beaten mixture of egg whites and sugar that has been baked slowly until it firms and turns pale golden; may be cooked or uncooked; used as a topping for pies and cakes.

Miltz
A spleen.

Mince
To slice into very fine particles.

Mohn
Poppy seed, used in hamantaschen at Purim, also used in baking of challah, rolls and bagel.

Mousse
A chilled dessert consisting chiefly of flavored and sweetened whipped cream.

Noodle
A flat pastry cut into long, thin strips and cooked in boiling water or broth.

Pan broil
To cook meat in a skillet, with just enough fat cooked out of the meat to prevent sticking.

Pan fry
To cook in a skillet with a minimum of fat.

Parboil
To cook partially in boiling water; cooking is usually completed by some other method.

Pare
To cut off the outer skin, usually from vegetables such as carrots or potatoes.

Pareve
Neither dairy nor meat, for example, fruit, fish and vegetables.

Parfait
A tall glass with a serving of a variety of flavored ice cream, layered, and topped with sauce and whipped cream.

Paste
Mixed foods mashed together; a jelly mixture or a flour mixture to be rolled out for pie crust or noodles.

Peel
To remove the outer layer of skin from fruit or vegetables.

Pilaf
A Middle Eastern dish made from boiled rice, seasonings and meat plus nuts and vegetables.

Pirogen or piroshki
Small dumplings filled with meat, fish or rice, and fried or baked.

Pit
To remove the seeds or stones from fruit.

Poach
To cook food gently in a seasoned liquid so that it will retain its shape.

Purée
To force cooked food through a food processor or strainer until it is smooth and light.

Ragout
A thick, well-seasoned meat stew.

Reduce
To cook a liquid over a high heat until it has reduced in volume and has become more concentrated in flavor.

Render
To remove fat from poultry and cook it until it reaches a liquid state.

Roast
To cook meat such as poultry in an open roasting pan in the oven.

Russel
A soured beet juice used especially during Passover to make borscht.

Sauce
Meat gelatinized in the roasting pan and thinned with water or broth; or it may be a complex mixture.

Sauté
To fry food in a small amount of fat, tossing it back and forth quickly.

Scald
To bring a liquid such as milk to simmering point; or to pour boiling water over vegetables and allow them to stand for a few minutes.

Scallion
An onion that has not developed a bulb.

Scallop
Thin slices of veal.

Schav
A soup made from sorrel grass or spinach.

Schmaltz
Rendered chicken or goose fat.

Scramble
To mix—such as combining the whites and yolks of eggs before cooking.

Sear
To brown the surface of meat quickly by subjecting it to a high temperature during the first few minutes of cooking.

Season
To add salt, pepper, spices or herbs in order to improve flavor.

Sherbet
A liquid mixture made with fruit flavor and frozen.

Shred
To cut or tear into thin strips with a grater or knife.

Sift
To put dry ingredients through a fine sieve.

Skewer
A long metal or wooden pin on which to cook meat and vegetables.

Steam
A method of cooking food on a rack by steam rather than by boiling; the water should not touch the food.

Stew
To simmer in liquid until tender.

Stir
To mix food with a circular motion in order to blend it and produce a uniform consistency.

Stock
Liquid in which meat, poultry, fish or vegetables have been cooked.

Stuff
To fill a cavity with chopped or minced ingredients combined with breadcrumbs.

Toast
To brown by means of direct heat or oven heat.

Torte
Any cake baked in a torte pan, especially one with a baked meringue topping; also a rich cake of several thin layers with filling between each layer.

Toss
To mix by lifting lightly, as a salad, usually using a fork and spoon so that the ingredients are adequately mixed.

Truss
To fasten into position with skewers and twine.

Veronique
A recipe in which grapes are used as an ingredient.

Whip
To beat vigorously, thus incorporating air into the food and increasing its volume.

GLOSSARY

THE following list includes equivalents or substitutes for ingredients and cookery terms that are commonly used in America (and this book), but which may be less well known to Australian readers.

AMERICAN	AUSTRALIAN
alligator pear	avocado
all-purpose flour	plain flour
almond extract	almond essence
American cheese	processed Cheddar cheese
baking sheet	baking tray
baking soda	bicarbonate of soda
beets	beetroot
Bermuda onion	white onion
bing cherries	black cherries
biscuit	scone
bouillon cubes	stock cubes
broiled/broiler	grilled/griller
Bundtform pan	round, fluted cake tin
cake/baking pan	cake tin
cake flour	plain flour
candied	glace (fruits)
cantaloupe	rockmelon
catsup	tomato sauce
celery-cabbage	Chinese cabbage
celery root	celeriac
confectioners' sugar	icing sugar
cookie press	biscuit cutter
cookies	biscuits
cornmeal	polenta
cornstarch	cornflour
corn syrup	liquid glucose
crock	earthenware jar
currant jelly	red currant jelly preserve
dash	pinch (of salt)

AMERICAN	AUSTRALIAN
Dutch oven	heavy iron saucepan with tight-fitting lid
extract	essence
flanken	top rib beef
food chopper	Moulinex food processor
gelatin, flavored	jelly crystals
gelatin, 1 envelope of	1 tablespoon gelatine
Graham crackers	Sunshine Holsum biscuits
granulated gelatin	gelatine
granulated sugar	sugar
green pepper	capsicum
griddle	frying pan
ground	mince/minced (meat)
halibut	jewfish
hard-cooked egg	hard-boiled egg
hip beef	forequarter beef
Kitchen Bouquet	barbecue sauce (substitute)
kumquat	cumquat
London broil	skirt steak
mixed candied fruit	mixed peel
molasses	treacle
navy beans	hericot beans
Nesselro	chocolate sprinkles
nutmeats	nuts
package	packet
pan	tin
paper toweling	absorbent paper
pare	peel
pie crusts	pie shells/pastry
pit	stone, seed, pip
potato starch	cornflour
powdered sugar	icing sugar
red pepper	cayenne pepper
refrigerator tray	freezer tray
roasted sweet peppers	pimientoes
Romano cheese	Romano, Parmesan or a hard cheese
salmon	groper
salted crackers	Salada biscuits
scallions	spring onions
seedless raisins	raisins
sherbet	water-based icecream
shredded coconut	dessicated coconut
short ribs	spare ribs
simple syrup	1 cup water and 1 cup sugar boiled for 2 mins.
skillet	frying pan
smelts	small fish, e.g. whitebait
sole	bream
soup greens	soup vegetables
Springerle rolling pin	rolling pin with embossed design

AMERICAN	AUSTRALIAN
springform pan	springform cake tin
squash	pumpkin
stew beef	gravy beef
stewing steak	chuck steak
(to) strain	sift
strain/strainer	sieve
summer squash	zucchini
wax paper	greaseproof paper
(to) whip, beat	(to) whisk
white horseradish	creamed horseradish
white raisins	sultanas
yellow squash	butternut

INDEX